THE QUILTED OBJECT

A Challenge for 2018!

Dorothy

THE QUILTED OBJECT

Ineke Berlyn

BATSFORD

First published in the UK in 2009 by
Batsford
10 Southcombe Street
London W14 0RA

An imprint of Anova Books Company Ltd

ISBN-13: 9781906388232

A CIP catalogue record for this book is available from the British
Library.

15 14 13 12 10 09
10 9 8 7 6 5 4 3 2 1

Repro by Rival Colour Ltd, UK
Printed by Craft Print Ltd, Singapore

This book can be ordered direct from the publisher at the
website: www.anovabooks.com, or try your local bookshop.

Distributed in the United States and Canada by Sterling
Publishing Co., 387 Park Avenue South, New York, NY 10016,
USA

CONTENTS

INTRODUCTION

Although I'm writing the words for this introduction while sitting on a beautiful coral sand beach in Bermuda, I would not class this book as your typical blockbuster beach read. Even so, this beach and the amazing turquoise sea could give anyone plenty of inspiration, as you can see from the accompanying pictures, sketchbook pages and subsequent piece of work. The message, therefore, is this: don't leave home without your camera and sketchbook and be inspired by what's in front of you and what's in your mind.

Right and below:

Elbow Beach, Bermuda.

Above:

'Bermuda Triangle', a 30-cm (12-in)
journal quilt inspired by the
sketchbook pages and the
photographs (opposite).

The Quilted Object includes a range of stitched objects and projects that have popped into my
head when I was having a moment away from landscape quilting. I am always tempted by
new materials, like Lutradur, and when in need of a little something, like a birthday card, I
like to try something different. A pile of old jeans inspired me to turn them into a fabulous
bag, and my own chickens and life in the countryside led to fun projects like making a
quilted chicken or a sheep. The thing that links all these projects is that they all involve
layering materials which, to me, makes it a quilt of some kind. The willingness to try new
things is an important part of developing ideas and to expand the uses of quilting techniques.

So, for those of you who enjoy experimenting with new materials and fabric decoration
techniques, I have included printing with Thermofax screens and dissolving silk screens, as
well as my explorations with Lutradur, which have produced some exciting results. In fact,
every chapter will touch on some of the endless possibilities of this versatile material.

New quilt groups are being formed everywhere, so I have included a few interesting and
successful group projects. Many exhibitions and competitions now have a separate category
for groups and this is a superb way to encourage people to work together.

Above:
An embellished diary cover for my
mini Filofax, made at a workshop
by Jenny Rolfe.

Writing a second book after the success of the first, *Landscape in Contemporary Quilts*, has proved a tough challenge. Time is getting more and more precious, not only for me, but for most of my readers as well, which is why you will find plenty of suggestions in this book for little quilted objects that can be made quickly, mostly with materials you can find around the house.

Recycling is becoming a topical subject these days and, having collected denim jeans for several years, I finally found a good use for them and complemented them with the T-shirts they were worn with by turning them into bags, purses and other 3-D items.

To finish each chapter, I have looked at some of the textile artists and quilters whose work inspired me. Hopefully, their thoughts and projects will also entice you into creating new and exciting work.

I know from your comments that the postcards contained in *Landscape in Contemporary Quilting* were very popular with the kids, so more ideas for making postcards for seasonal and other occasions can be found in chapter 3. In the words of the famous British traditional quilter, Amy Emms, 'Pass it on! Especially to your children and grandchildren.' Most of us were taught the basics by our mothers and grandmothers and, following on in the same tradition, I plead with you to make a concerrted effort to pass on the joy of stitching to the young ones. Keep encouraging your youngsters and see how they can surprise themselves and you with their creativity. In turn, they might even inspire you!

Below: Postcard made from left-over bits of denim.

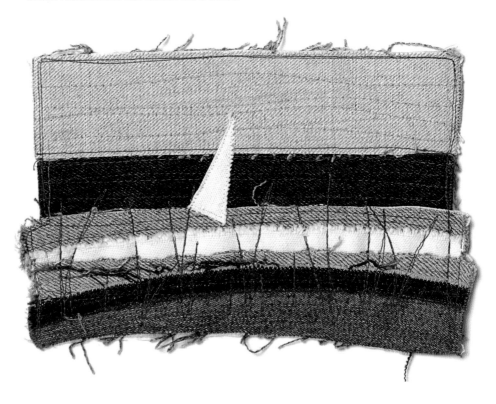

1 JOURNAL QUILTS AND SKETCHBOOKS

If you look up the word 'journal' in a dictionary, you will find that it is a book in which a record of a person's daily activities is noted, a diary of events or news; in navigational terms, it is a logbook or daily register of the ship's course and distance, the journal-box being the metal case in which the journal moves. The word comes from the French 'jour', meaning 'day', which in turn is derived from the Latin for day: dies – diem – diurnal.

Much of our historical knowledge is based on the diaries that individuals kept throughout the ages, recording what may have seemed very ordinary events but giving us a unique window through which we can look into their lives. The Chinese, Romans, Greeks and Egyptians all left written work detailing their daily lives.

Below:
A pile of sketchbooks, each one individually wrapped in its own colourful quilted cover.

I've been keeping journal sketchbooks throughout the last few years. Initially, I considered them to be one of the less enjoyable requirements needed to pass the City and Guilds exams in Patchwork and Quilting. Nowadays – probably because I am no longer obliged to keep a journal – they are among my most treasured pieces of work. In some ways, they are even more precious than the actual pieces that have been created as a result of keeping them. My journals are the kind of legacy that hopefully can be passed on to my grandchildren and their children – along, of course, with the quilts and other pieces of work.

All artists keep sketchbooks and diaries – so why not start one yourself?

Inspired by Theme

Below:

Judith Hill's sketchbook shows how the Scottish landscape inspired her that month.

Opposite:

The journal quilt – inspired by the Scottish landscape – is made by stitching raw-edge strips of fabric onto fusible wadding. The combination of fine machine stitching and simple hand stitching provides plenty of visual interest.

Yours does not have to be a journal in the strict sense of the word, but it is important to commit yourself to a regular daily, weekly or monthly art-based exercise. If you do, this will most certainly become a rich source of inspiration. Give yourself a theme, such as the first day of each month or every Sunday, or take a word that can run like a red line through your sketchbook or journal – for example, the sun, the moon, your garden, the seasons or the weather – and then train yourself to take a little time regularly to explore and play.

Here is a selection of words that I have given my students as themes for their journals, all related in some way to the landscape or earth: trees, sea, birds, sky, flora, hills, seasons, moon, sun, stars, maps, colour, urban, grass and contours.

Involve your children or grandchildren in your creative activity – start them off and let them roll. Giving them a tiny sketchbook is a brilliant way of encouraging them to take their first steps into art. Let them decide on a theme and, together, work your way through it. You never know what might come of it.

Your Little Sketchbook

Find a little sketchbook, about 10 cm (4 in) square, suitable for keeping a journal, a sort of mini scrapbook, small enough to keep in your handbag.

The aim behind this is to help you to train your mind to think creatively by gradually building up a collection of ideas and thoughts that might form the basis of a design.

If you keep your book in a bag or a box, together with a small pair of scissors, a glue stick, a pencil, a pen and a small paint box and brush (and maybe even a little pot of water), you will always have everything at hand to complete a page or two.

It won't take you a lot of time to add a little bit to your sketchbook every now and then. You might intend to do a daily stint, but, as with all good intentions, more often than not you will find that something comes up that needs your attention, so that little bit of art gets pushed back and forgotten. But then it's Sunday; you're enjoying a cup of tea or coffee; you look outside, and suddenly inspiration hits you. Of course, you have your 'toolkit' handy and will be able to start straight away!

Putting pen to a glaringly white sheet of paper can be quite frightening, so start by giving the first few pages a wash with watercolour. Leave them to dry and then perhaps add a background pattern with some soft stamps or a sponge.

Right:

'Ready, Sketch, Go' bag with a small 10-cm (4-in) sketchbook, gluestick, paints, mini jar, scissors, pen and pencil. This simple small calico bag holds all the equipment I need to fill up pages in my mini sketchbook.

Above:
A sketchbook with notes and
samples that all relate to the final
quilted postcard 'Tulips', shown top
right of the sketchbook page.

As you are most probably a textile person, you might like to add some texture with needle
and thread and experiment by altering some traditional embroidery stitches. Below are some
examples of ways you might begin to fill your sketchbook:

- To add a bit of sparkle, you can glue buttons, beads or sequins to the odd page or two
- Perhaps you see something in a newspaper or magazine that catches your eye – if so, stick
  it in
- If you've visited a museum, theatre or the like, use the ticket and a few words to fill a
  couple of pages
- While on holiday, you might find an hour or so to doodle or paint
- If you receive a note with an unusual stamp or an attractive birthday or anniversary card,
  this could go in your book
- Perhaps you might record a nice poem you've come across
- While you wait for a doctor or dentist, why not rip their magazines to bits or doodle a
  page with a nice pattern?
- Try using a craft knife to cut out a window, allowing you to look through to the next
  page
- Or perhaps you could cut a sequence of pages to form the different layers of a landscape
- … and if you've made a mess of a page, don't rip it out! Cover it with paint, stamp on it
  or glue something over it and start again.

Journal Quilts

Making a 'Journal Quilt' has become tremendously popular as a form of group project. It all started in 1999, when the American quilter, Jeanne Williamson, began making a small 'once a week' quilt to tell the story of her life. This inspired the director of the International Quilt Festival to set up the Journal Quilt Project. The size was set at 21.5 x 28 cm (8½ x 11 in) – standard A4 – and the project encouraged an ongoing free-form exercise in creativity, specifically planned to stretch quilt artists by encouraging them to try new methods and to experiment with colour, image, composition, materials and techniques. Artists were required to make one quilt a month from January till September. More information on the Journal Quilt Project can be found on the official website: http://www.quiltart.com/journals/.

Below:

Two A4-size journal quilts – for June and August – made of painted Lutradur, appliquéd and stitched.

In the United Kingdom, the Contemporary Quilt Group – part of the Quilters' Guild of the British Isles – also started a monthly Journal Quilt for its members and each quarter pictures of the completed A4 quilts were posted to an internet site. For me, this was the perfect excuse to explore Lutradur, a new material (more of which can be found later, on page 46). I chose 'Where am I on the first day of each month?' as my theme.

Below:
A set of four 30-cm (12-in) square
silk quilts inspired by the Scilly
Isles. By Jennie Wood.

First pin 2 strips of fabric on top of a square of wadding with backing fabric and then stitch.

Once strips 1 and 2 are stitched, flip the piece over and press. Return to the front and add strip 3 as in step 1.

Once all the strips are stitched, the piece is ready for additional machine or hand quilting.

Quilt-as-you-go Technique

The following year's challenge was based on producing a 30 cm (12 in) square quilt. I decided to go back to basics and look at the colours each month. I made each square by the quilt-as-you-go method, which is a quick technique, using straight strips of fabric, and suitable for smaller projects.

1. Start with a 31.5 cm (12½ in) square backing fabric, topped by a 31.5 cm (12½ in) square of wadding.

2. Decide on a sequence of strips of fabrics. I used dyed linen and cotton fabrics, based on the colours of the sky and reflecting the weather that particular month. These were cut into strips of varying widths.

3. Place the bottom strip directly onto the background (wadded) fabric, and then place the next strip, right sides together, on top of this; pin to secure and stitch through all four layers with the sewing machine. By stitching through all the layers you are, in effect, quilting the block as you go along.

4. Next, flip the second strip over and iron or fingerpress the seam.

5. Now place the following strip along the unstitched edge of the second strip, again right sides together, and repeat the process.

This is a very quick and easy way to create simple quilted squares. I then added a little more hand and machine quilting, to make things a bit more interesting.

Some of the best journal quilts are shown throughout this chapter.

Ideas for Group Projects

Quilt groups of all kinds are becoming more and more popular. Women of all ages are getting together with kindred spirits to fulfil the need to be creative, particularly by working with textiles. Many of these new quilt groups call themselves 'house groups', as they meet weekly or monthly in each other's homes. To keep interest going and to avoid it becoming more 'bitch' than 'stitch', the groups are trying to find projects that involve everyone and ensure there is something to work on and to 'show and tell' at each meeting.

One method, developed while working with staff and patients at Primrose Hospice, has proved a very useful way of working in a group. Together, we designed a quilt that could be made in strips and was based on a picture taken from a calendar by the Dutch artist Ton Schulten. One member of the staff designed a happy and bright pattern in five sections and each day of the week the group made their own strip, using fabrics out of a big box filled with a wide range of scrap fabrics.

The finished strips were about 75 cm (30 in) long and the widths varied between 30 cm (12 in) and 62.5 cm (25 in). When the strips were all pieced, mainly by hand, they were individually backed with wadding and backing fabric before the quilting could begin. Many of the patients were more familiar with embroidery than quilting, so they really enjoyed adding little flowers, birds and so on.

Having finished quilting the strips, we cut back the wadding and then stitched them together: we stitched the top layers together first along the long seams, butting up the wadding, and then finished by neatly folding over the seams at the back and slip-stitching them. I took the quilt home to square it off and bind it, folding the binding all the way around and stitching it onto the reverse side, adding a sleeve at the top from which to hang the work.

The quilt now has pride of place in their dayroom and really brightens the place up.

Above:
Group quilt made by patients and staff at the Primrose Hospital in Bromsgrove, England.

Organizing Your Own Challenge

It is important to choose a manageable format for this kind of challenge. Anything larger than 30 cm (12 in) square will be difficult to store, let alone complete on a regular basis. Moreover, if you or your group are aiming to display all of the entries, you will need a very large exhibition space.

Postcard size, or any size that can be stored and displayed in photograph albums, is perfect for a challenge of this type. A4, A5 or A6 display albums are all readily available from stationary stores. Alternatively, why not opt for the very latest in display technology and use one of the new compact digital picture display systems to give a continuous slide show of your complete series.

Not everybody is happy to work within these formal restrictions and some might want to experiment with 3-D items:

- Make a miniature book each month
- Make a bag, always following the same pattern but with different fabrics and techniques
- Perhaps the challenge could be to make a doll – trying to find a different pattern each month or season.

If you are looking for unusual fabrics, a great way to start is by dyeing your own and perhaps using only the materials dyed in one particular session for each quilt.

Inspiration

For instant inspiration, I always tend to take a look at one of my sketchbooks or thumb through a colourful magazine, such as *Quilting Arts* or *Cloth Paper Scissors*, or a mixed media book. Once a theme has been found, try to work spontaneously and go with the first thought that comes into your mind. Working small is all about responding to your intuition. Your instinct tells you what you like in a split second and once you learn to recognise and react to that, you will find plenty of inspiration in the things that you see everyday.

I try to sit down and doodle some days, but in reality it's only when I'm on holiday that there is enough time to lose myself in a sketchbook or a design project. I think that's why so many of my pieces come from inspiration found in France.

Below:

Sketchbook pages that are painted with leftover yellow procion dye and mono printed with red acrylic paint. The right hand page has been cut into a tulip shape.

Sketchbook pages inspired by the
sunflower fields in France.
From the left it records a dyeing
sequence, photographs, rough
sketches with a marker pen,
thermofax screen prints of leaves
and lines of the poem 'The
Sunflowers' by Mary Oliver.

Design Development

I was lucky enough to take a five-day course with the
American quilter Bob Adams, exploring new ways to
approach machine stitching. With my own interest in
landscape, I was attracted to his work at the 2007 Festival of
Quilts, where he exhibited moonlit landscapes and dark,
discharged pieces, enhanced with clever machine quilting
(see page 35).

On the first day of the course, my starting point was the
simple pomegranate I had brought along for inspiration. A
whole series of small quilted pieces grew from this and along
the way I discovered a new free-machine technique.

Left:

'Tournesol', the finished sunflower wallhanging after design development.

Project – a Simple Shape

The first objective is to explore a simple shape, such a piece of fruit, a flower, a shell or any other favourite object, by making simple line drawings:

- Try drawing a contour without looking at the paper and without lifting your pencil
- Repeat this with your other hand
- Next, draw a line with a pencil while looking at the object properly
- Draw it again, this time with a pen
- Sketch a suggested shape by scrawling nice curvy shapes with pen or pencil
- Now hold both a pen and a pencil in your fist; loosen up; step back, and sketch again
- Try this with three or four different thickness of marker pen, fine liners and pencils held together with an elastic band – be free and rough!

And keep playing – play a lot! Try different strokes, straight lines, figures of eight, zigzags and so on. Perhaps you could really simplify your drawing, going back to the start and trying again. After about an hour, you should have enough explorations to start you off stitching.

Now take a look through the pages of your sketchbook and choose your favourite drawing.

Right:

Sketches of pomegranates made by holding a black pencil, fineliner and thick marker together in one hand. The exercise was used at the Bob Adams' sessions.

1. Make a quilt sandwich with a white cotton top – about 50 cm (19½ in) square – and put black thread in your machine, with a mono filament in your bobbin (a full bobbin with invisible thread should last you a good few hours of stitching).

2. Put your embroidery or darning foot on and drop the feed dogs on your sewing machine. The feed dogs are the little teeth underneath the plate that grip the fabric. You might need to look in your handbook to find the switch that drops them. Alternatively, with some machines you can put a thin plate on top to enable you to move your fabric around freely.

3. Sit comfortably behind your sewing machine (to help your posture, place a doorstop wedge underneath the back of your sewing machine, which helps relax the shoulders). Duplicate the drawing, using the needle as your pen and moving the fabric as you draw. Make a rough sketch first before emphasising the thicker lines by going over them several times.

My first attempt was quite tight, but bit by bit the drawings started to loosen up. I managed some quite big stitches by using the basting function on my machine, which misses every other stitch, and moving the fabric quite fast.

Right:

Free-machine quilting with black thread on a white background. It was based on the pomegranate sketches opposite – with a few red dots added for contrast.

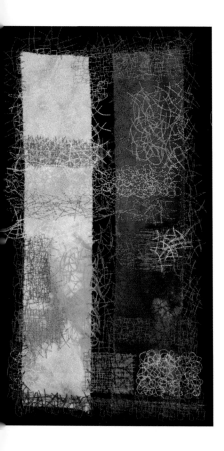

Play with Colour

Having explored lines in simple black and white, you can now use the same basic technique, but this time start playing around with colour. You will find that you are able to alter the value of the colour of the fabric with different threads and stitchery. This sample piece, in which a strip of warm red fabric was placed next to a strip of cool green, was quilted with a variety of threads in different colours to show how they react together. It all goes back to the basic rules of the colour wheel: using orange thread on blue fabric will warm the fabric up, for example, while green thread will cool down a red piece of cloth and so on.

Sticking with the pomegranate, I cut some strips out of a warm pinkish fabric, which was backed with Bondaweb, keeping the surrounding fabric for use on another piece of work. I also cut a couple of pomegranate shapes out of the cooler green.

By looking at my drawings, I found a good 'cross hatch' stitch pattern that I used as an all-over quilt pattern. See if you can find your own mark-making stitch.

I also love drawing with text and, by altering the size and the angle of the writing, you can create interesting patterns and textures.

I fused some of the pomegranates on white and the others on a black background. Next, I started 'colouring' them in with my new found cross-hatch pattern; intensifying the darker areas with pinks and red and highlighting the light spots with a very pale pink. The writing and few sketch lines in black add just enough interest and contrast.

Bob Adams' other specialist area is discharge and bleaching and so, using a special brush-pen that can be filled with bleach, I continued the experiment by sketching more pomegranates onto a special black discharge cotton sateen and enhancing these with more free-machine stitching.

All these pieces look lovely in simple black or white square frames or can be finished off and glued onto a box canvas as described on page 85.

Above right:
Developing a new free-machine pattern on appliquéd pomegranates.

Right:
Further developments on black fabric, creating areas of light and dark with intense machine stitching with different coloured threads.

Top left:
Sample piece showing the effects of machine quilting on cool and warm colours.

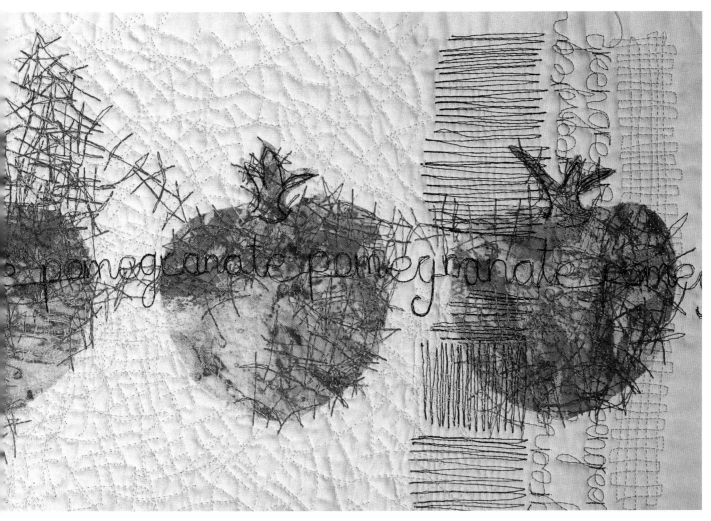

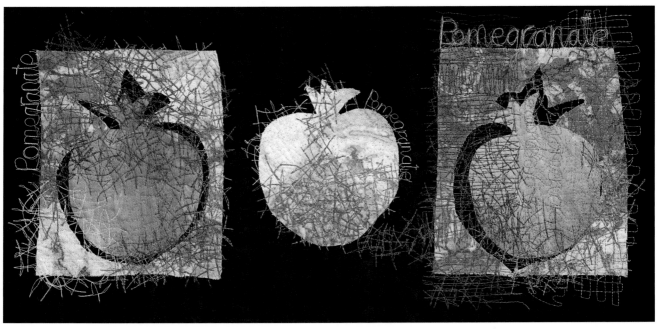

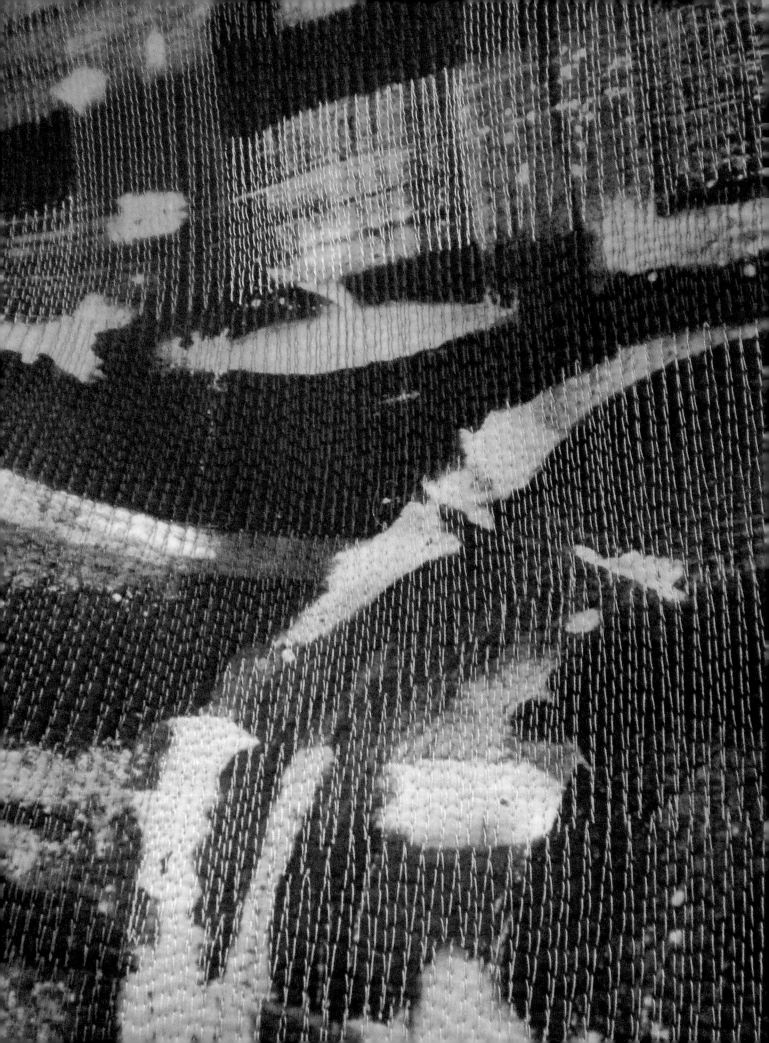

Design Tip

Sometimes somebody shows you a little trick that is so useful and easy that you find yourself using it again and again. This is one of them.

When putting together a landscape you might want to create a random uneven pattern to use as a row of distant hills in a landscape, for example, or the top of a stone wall in the foreground, but it is difficult to do this simply by just cutting it with a pair of scissors. Instead, try the following:

1. Take a length of fabric (or try it with some tissue paper first),
    about 25 cm (10 in) long and about 10 cm (4 in) wide.

2. Pleat it together tightly.

3. Next, twist it in the middle, a bit like the top of a sweet wrapper.

4. Cut through the twist with a sharp pair of scissors. You might need a pair of extra hands to hold the other side, but perhaps you will be able to hold the top between your index and middle fingers and the bottom between your thumb and ring fingers.

Depending on the way you cut the fabric – either straight, at an angle or haphazard and wriggly – you will get a different result every time.

Now you have got not one perfect hillside, but two, which can be placed on top of each other to create an even greater sense of distance. Again, you will discover there are lots more variations, according to how tightly you pleat or fold the fabric – just have a play!

If you are using your strip for an appliqué landscape, you might want to put some Bondaweb on the back, but take the backing paper off before pleating it. When cut, it is ready to iron on. If you have forgotten to put some fusible web on, just spray the piece with 505 spray glue before you position it.

Left:
Detail of a piece by Bob Adams, showing how the colour of the thread interacts with the different backgrounds.

Below:
Create random ragged edges by pleating, twisting and cutting strips of fabric.

2 COLOUR ON FABRIC

For me, one of the most important considerations when creating quilts or any quilted object is the colours. Only by dyeing fabric can you get just the colour you want or produce a new, surprising colour that can inspire you in your creative work. Dyeing fabrics is a vital part of any quilting project, whether it's a quilted bag, a doll or a book cover.

Dyeing Fabric

Recently, I have found that by adding salt to the dyeing process I can achieve the very deep dark browns, blacks and navy that were almost impossible to create without the addition of salt. To dye a series of fabrics that vary from dark to light in one colour follow the instructions below.

Materials and Equipment

- Rubber gloves, apron and utensils (that are only used for dyeing)
- Face mask
- 8 plastic cups or watertight plastic bags
- 8 pieces of fabric, about 20 cm (8 in) square (you might like to include some fabrics with interesting textures)
- Some cotton thread, wound into skeins
- Soda solution of 225 g (8 oz) of soda ash (sodium carbonate; available from mail order dye supplier or a swimming pool supply store), dissolved in 4.5 litres (1 gallon) of hot water
- Procion cold-water dye powder
- Salt-water solution (100 g/4 oz salt in 1 litre/2 pints of hot water) to mix with the dyes

1. Soak the fabrics for at least one hour in the soda solution. I often prepare them the night before.

2. Make up the dye as follows: mix 1 teaspoon of dye powder with a little very warm water to make a smooth paste, and then add salt-water solution to make up to 250 ml (8 fl oz), preparing the solution in a measuring cup. Choose a primary colour or mix colours to achieve the colour you desire – of course, you can purchase any colour ready-mixed.

Right: Bunch of fabrics dyed in a rainbow of colours. They will give you a rich supply of fabrics for your quilting projects.

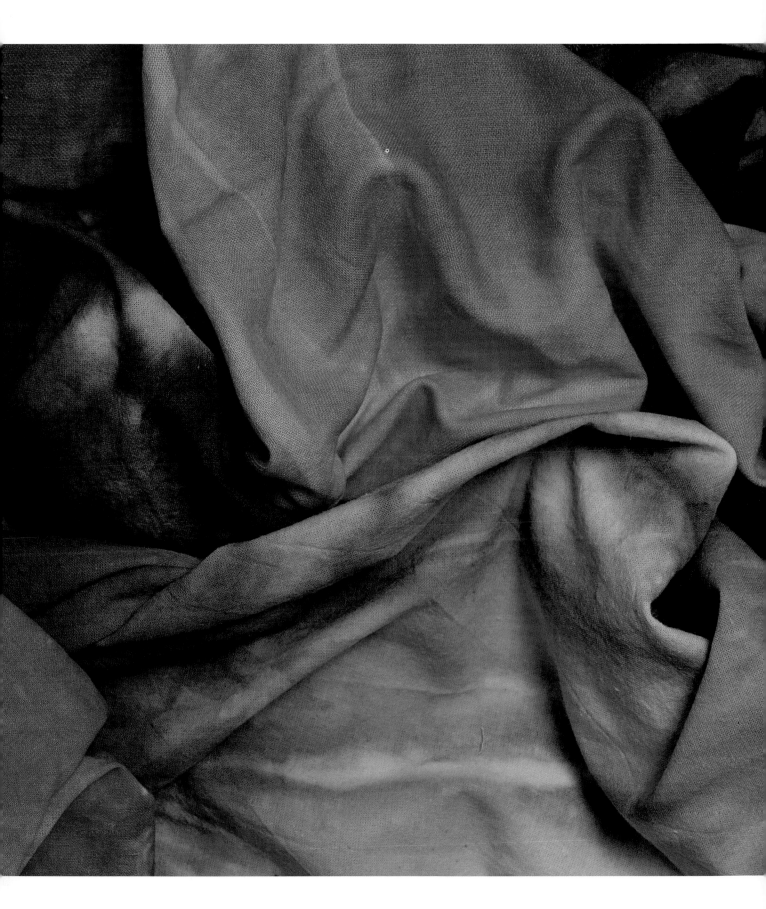

3. Line up plastic cups or bags in a row, marking them from 1 to 8.

4. Take your dye solution and 500 ml (16 fl oz) of salt-water solution.

5. Pour half the dye solution into the cup marked number 1 and press a soaked piece of fabric into this.

6. Pour 125 ml (4 fl oz) of salt-water solution into the original measuring cup. You now have 250 ml (8 fl oz) again with a slightly weaker dye solution.

7. Pour half of this half-strength solution into cup number 2 and add fabric.

8. Again, top up your measuring cup with 125 ml (4 fl oz) of salt-water; pour half of this into cup number 3 and add fabric.

9. Continue to repeat the process until all eight cups are filled.

10. Throw away the remaining solution as it will be very weak, or use it to give some pages of your sketchbook a light wash with a big paintbrush.

11. Leave the fabric to cure overnight or for at least 3 hours (24 hours for turquoise), before rinsing and then washing with a chlorine-free detergent.

12. Leave the fabrics to dry and then iron them.

When you arrange your fabrics in a row, you will see a subtle but very obvious gradation from dark to light.

Below:

A series of fabrics going from light to dark, dyed using the gradation dyeing process.

Multi-coloured Dyeing

Now from very controlled to very haphazard dyeing, something I much prefer. The main requirement for this is a spot of nice weather, because I like to do this outside in the garden.

Materials and Equipment

- Rubber gloves, apron and utensils that are only used for dyeing
- Face mask
- A large piece of strong plastic, measuring 1 x 1.5 m (40 x 60 in) or a large cat litter tray
- 6 jam jars
- Sunshine
- 1–2 m (1–2 yd) of medium-thickness cotton fabric, soaked in soda solution
- Salt-water solution
- Procion cold-water dyes – yellow, red, cerise, royal, turquoise, navy, black and green

1. Spread the plastic sheet on the lawn, gravel or patio (don't worry, the dye will wash off), preferably on a slight incline.

2. Place your piece of fabric on the plastic and gently concertina it into a sausage shape. If you are using a large tray, arrange your fabric in a wave pattern as shown in the picture below.

3. Prepare your dyes by mixing each into a separate jar and topping up the jars with salt-water solution. Note that once the dyes have been mixed with salt water they will remain at their best for about 30 minutes.

Right:
A tray of rainbow-dyed fabric, curing in the sun.

4. I would start with yellow at the highest point, if you have managed to find a slightly
    sloping site, or on one side, if you're dyeing in a tray, because this will keep the yellow
    clean. I squeeze the dye into the top end of the fabric, also leaving some white bits.

5. Next, you can either mix some red in with the yellow dye to create an orange and then
    pour this next to the yellow or you can pour red on the fabric and mix the colours with
    gloved hands.

6. Now add some more red to create a red patch.

7. Add the cerise, again either mixing part of the red dyed area with cerise by hand or
    adding cerise to the red dye jar first.

8. Add more cerise to make a cerise patch of fabric and then blend in royal blue, which will
    make a purple.

9. Continue to make the next area plain royal blue and here you might want to create some green by mixing equal amounts of yellow and blue in a jar.

10. From green go into turqoise followed by navy and black to give you some dark fabrics.

11. If you want, you can make further colour mixtures, but be careful if you have a dark colour on your gloves and rinse them first before attacking the yellow and reds!

12. Now roll the plastic up tightly. Secure the top and bottom with clothes pegs and leave the roll to cure in the sun for a day or so. This is especially important if you have used turquoise, as you will need to leave it for 24 hours.

13. The next day, rinse it out under the tap outside.

14. After rinsing, give it a quick wash in the machine with some soft chlorine-free detergent; let it dry and then iron it.

You will now have the most fantastic and useful piece of fabric. It's always totally unpredictable how it will turn out, but the result is usually absolutely brilliant.

Right:
These fabrics have been pleated tightly before dye has been poured onto them, producing interesting markings.

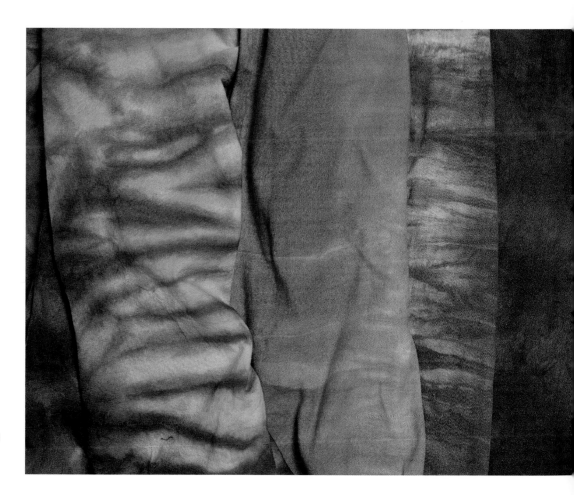

Above: Inspirational sunset.

Right:
Large wallhanging 'Sunset' made with a selection of hand-dyed fabrics and quilted with the words of one of the 'Love Spell' poems by Kathleen Raine.

Far right:
'Full Moon' by Bob Adams. Black fabric has been discharged and overpainted with orange dye. Bands of zig-zag machine stitching have created interesting horizontal lines.

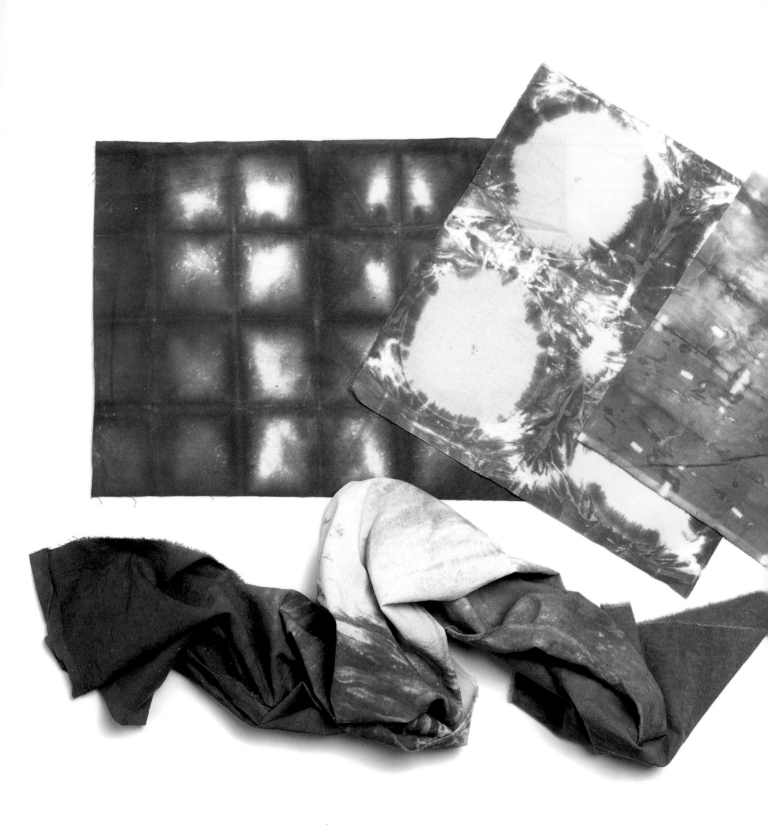

Indigo

Indigo is a very natural fabric colouring. It is one of the worlds' oldest natural dyes, its use dating back more than five thousand years. Before the 20th century, every blue fabric was dyed with indigo. Indigo producing plants (*Indigofera tinctoria*) can be found almost everywhere in the world and, although we associate it with exotic countries, such as India, Japan and China, a similar plant, named woad (*Isatis tinctoria*) can be grown in Europe. Because of its chemical make-up, indigo has the ability to dye every type of natural fabric or yarn, be it animal or vegetable, in an identical blue colour.

Woad takes months of fermentation to produce its dye, but *Indigofera tinctoria* only traditionally needed soaking for a couple of days before oxygen was added by beating it with sticks. The blue paste that was left over was perfect for drying into a pigment that could be stored and transported.

Most natural dyes need a 'mordant' to become permanent, but indigo needs an alkaline dye vat, made up of caustic soda and hydrogen. When fabric is dipped in an indigo vat, it will come out yellow and it is through the contact with the air that the colour oxidises into the typical indigo blue. Darker colours are obtained by dipping the fabric several times into the vat.

One can find indigo-dyed textiles in cultures all over the world. Resist techniques must be used to create patterns on the cloth. This is because indigo oxidizes on contact with the air, so it is difficult to print patterns directly onto the cloth. Instead, patterns can be painted onto the fabric with wax or pastes, or shibori techniques, such as pleating, tying or stitching, can be used to ensure that certain areas remain white after the fabric is dipped into the indigo dye vat.

These days, we could hardly envisage life without indigo in the form of the famous blue jeans. In 1873, Levi Strauss started to use the thick cotton twill produced in the French town of Nimes, 'serge de Nimes', to make strong blue work trousers for the cowboys. These became known as 'blue de Nimes', shortened to 'blue denim', and eventually became an essential part of modern life.

To make your own vat of indigo, you will need:
• Caustic soda
• Sodium hydrosulphite
• Safety glasses
• Heavy duty rubber gloves
• Dust mask
• Protective coat
• Bucket with a lid
• Another sunny day

Above:

A selection of indigo- and shibori-dyed fabrics.

Top:
Fabric smocked and painted with batik wax before being dipped in indigo.

Bottom:
Leaves dipped in indigo are placed on one half of a calico square, then folded and rubbed to give a double print.

1. Pour in 4 litres (approximately 7 pints) of warm water into a deep, 10 litre (2½ gallon) tub or bucket with a lid.

2. Dissolve 30 g (1¼ oz) of caustic soda in 1 litre (1¾ pt) of cold water and then add this to the bucket and stir.

3. Very carefully, dissolve 20 g (scant 1 oz) of hydros, or sodium hydrosulphite, in 1 litre (1¾ pt) of cold water and add this to the bucket, stirring again.

4. Finally, dissolve 20 g (scant 1 oz) of indigo vat 60% grains in 500 ml (16 fl oz) of warm water in a plastic disposable container, stirring very gently so as not to let too much oxygen into the mixture.

5. Now very gently pour this into the side of the vat and then add another 3.5 litres (6¼ pints) of warm water.

6. Cover the vat and leave it to ferment for an hour or so.

7. To start dyeing your fabrics and threads, prepare some space outside. This process can be quite messy and smelly, which is why it really is a job for a nice day.

8. Using strong rubber gloves and tongs (remember there is caustic soda in this mixture), slightly dampen your fabric and dip it gently into the vat, holding it in the liquid for a minute or so before gently lifting it out.

9. When you hang the fabric out you will see the magical transformation from yellow to a gorgeous aqua, through to a definite indigo.

10. If you want to achieve a darker colour, dip your cloth in the dye vat again and again.

11. After a while, the results will become lighter as your vat becomes exhausted, due to the oxygen that is added each time you dip your fabrics.

12. The colour and the intensity depends on the many variables that you cannot control, such as the hardness or softness of your water, the humidity in the air, the temperature outside, how much air gets into your vat and the make-up of your fabric. But is it this unpredictability that makes indigo dyeing so interesting, ensuring that no two pieces of fabric will ever be the same.

13. If you have folded or pleated your fabric, dip it and then, once you have lifted it out, leave it folded till it is dry before you unwrap it and rinse, wash and dry.

14. Once all the fabrics are blue, rinse them under the cold tap and wash them in a chlorine-free detergent.

Safety Precautions

Caustic soda and sodium hydrosulphite are corrosive chemicals that can cause severe burns to the eyes and skin. Especially rigorous safety precautions therefore need to be taken to avoid skin and eye contact. Safety glasses, heavy duty rubber gloves, dust mask and lab coat must be worn when handling the chemicals. You must also make sure that no children or other vulnerable people risk coming into contact with the chemicals.

Printing the Easy Way

Printing or bleaching fabrics you've either bought or dyed can be as easy or complicated as you choose to make it. If you look around your house, I'm sure you'll find all sorts of textured materials that can be used for printed or bleached patterns. One of the simplest things to make prints with is bubble wrap. Starting with ordinary, but thick, bleach and pieces of bubble wrap, you can create stunning printed fabrics. I'm sure you've kept the odd piece of bubble wrap to satisfy that bubble popping urge, so be brave and do something new with it!

Make sure you have plenty of different cotton or other natural fabrics at hand, because the results are so quick and are different every time. Black fabrics can give interesting results, because the dyes used to produce them come from a range of colours. Different blacks, combined with different qualities of bleach, will therefore yield widely varied effects, ranging from white to burnt orange or greenish hues.

Materials and Equipment

- Pieces of coloured cotton fabric – bought or dyed
- An A4 piece of bubble wrap (you might experiment with a selection of pieces, with small, medium or large bubbles)
- Thick household bleach
- 2.5 cm (1 in) household paintbrush
- Plastic-covered worktop in a well-ventilated room
- Household gloves and face mask

From left to right:
Squares of dyed fabric from left to right; one is plain dyed; one is printed with corks and anti-slip matting, one is printed with two sizes of bubble wrap, and one is bleached out with large bubble wrap.

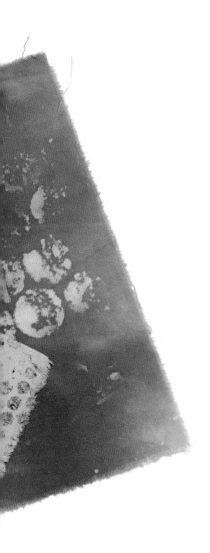

1. First protect your workspace with a sheet of plastic and then spread your coloured cotton fabric over it.

2. Pour some bleach on a saucer and, using a small household paintbrush, brush the textured side of the bubble wrap with bleach.

3. Gently press the bleach-covered side of the bubble wrap on the fabric.

4. Lift the bubble wrap and you will see the bleach doing its work.

5. When you feel that enough of the colour has discharged, submerge the fabric in a large bucket full of clean water to stop the bleaching action.

6. Squeeze the fabric well and then rinse and wash in a neutral washing liquid.

7. Leave it to dry and then iron it.

Textured patterns can be bleached or printed randomly or to a more regular design. You do not, of course, need to confine yourself to bubble wrap, but if you want to keep the round theme, you could try using wine corks or empty toilet roll holders. By cutting patterns out of the corks – sorry, you will need to drink yet another bottle – you can build up an interesting collection of simple patterns. Rubber stamps, carpet underlay or stamps made by gluing wooden coffee stirrers onto a block can all provide different textures to work with. Simple thin kitchen sponges can be cut into squares to make textured print blocks.

When all the bleached fabrics are washed, dried and ironed, you now have the choice of over-dyeing the fabrics or printing them with the same textural surfaces with which you bleached them. If you use the same bubble wrap, you can create brilliant fabrics that will all work together.

To dye the fabrics again, you will need to rinse and wash them, as in step 6, but it is not necessary to dry them. Instead, you can soak them into a solution of 1 cup (225 g/8 oz) of soda ash (sodium carbonate) dissolved in 4.5 litres (1 gallon) of water for about an hour. Mix one teaspoon of procion dye powder in your chosen colour along with 100 ml (3½ fl oz) of water. Place your pieces of fabric in a plastic tray and pour the dye mix over it. Leave it to cure for another hour or two – only turquoise needs 24 hours to take effect – then rinse and wash.

The pattern you bleached out will come out much lighter than the surrounding areas.

Safety Precautions

Working with bleach – even ordinary household bleach – will expose you to the dangerous fumes it gives off. Some of the very strong bleaches now available to clean all kinds of dirt off your bathroom tiles should really come with a gas mask. It's therefore a very good idea to kit yourself out with a face mask designed to protect the lungs while working with bleaches and other toxic fumes.

Printing with Paints

It is preferable to use special fabric paints for printing, as these have the correct consistency. Alternatively, you can mix acrylic paints with a fabric medium, but be sure to have a look at the manufacturers' instructions. Whichever paints you use, these will normally need to be ironed to set them and make them permanent. All the printing techniques described on pages 40–41 can be used extremely satisfactorily with paints.

To avoid colours appearing too harsh, it is a good idea to blend two or three together roughly before painting the mixture on the bubble side of the plastic wrap.

You can also cut out shapes, such as circles or squares, out of the bubble wrap. To make your patterns even more interesting, you might like to make templates out of sticky-backed plastic, cutting them to the same shape and size as your existing circles or squares. The bubble wrap and plastic 'resist' templates can then be used together to create positive and negative patterns on your fabric.

Now paint the bubble wrap (make sure you wash and rinse it thoroughly if it has been used for a previous printing job) with the prepared paints and start printing your fabric. I prefer to use colours that are a few shades lighter or darker than the background fabric. This not only helps to create a more subtle effect, but it has the added advantage that any mistakes are not so obvious.

To make a range of matching fabrics, you can cut six pieces:
• Leave one piece plain
• Bleach the second piece
• Bleach and over-dye the third piece
• Print the fourth piece
• Bleach and print the fifth piece
• Bleach, over-dye and print the sixth.

This simple method will give you an instant stock of textured fabrics for use in a wide variety of projects.

Printing with a Dissolving Silk Screen

It was my friend and tutor, Edwina Mackinnon, who introduced me to the process of printing with a dissolving silk screen. It can be a little time-consuming but worth it as it has such delightfully unpredictable and interesting results.

For this project, I used a linen/viscose fabric, but any natural fabric, such as cotton, linen or silk, would be suitable.

Materials and Equipment

- Wooden-framed silk screen
  (if it's a new frame, treat the wood with a couple of coats of wood varnish to protect against the wet)
- Squeegee (a rubber-edged tool used for grouting tiles and available from DIY stores)
- Manutex (a thickening agent)
- Procion dye powder
- 1-2 m (3–6 ft) of cotton or linen fabric
- Soda ash or washing soda
- Clean spray bottle (you can use an old detergent spray bottle as long as it's thoroughly cleaned)
- 1 m (3 ft) square sheet plastic
- An old sheet
- Pins

1. You start by soaking the fabric in a soda-ash solution overnight and drying it. Do not rinse, as the soda is needed to make the dye colourfast.

2. At the same time, mix some Manutex thickening agent with water to make a paste. This is best left overnight in the refrigerator to get the right consistency.

3. The next day, you can prepare your screen. For each dye colour, mix a small teaspoon of procion dye powder with about 50 ml (2 fl oz.) of water in a glass jar. I used cerise, red and yellow to create the warm reds and oranges for my dress. To make the coloured pastes, I used disposable plastic dessert dishes, each filled with three tablespoons of the Manutex paste and mixed small teaspoons of dye into each of these to get the right depth of colour. Keep the rest of the Manutex paste, as you will need it to print with later.

4. Now you are ready to paint the screens. Place a wooden screen printing frame screen side up and, using a small plastic spoon, draw shapes with the paste on the top of the screen. Colours can be mixed on the screen or in the bowls. When you are finished, you can create extra texture by placing bits of bubble wrap or other objects into the dye paste.

Below:

Cotton bag printed with a dissolving screen.

5. You need to leave it to dry out in a warm place on top of a big cat-litter tray or a sheet of plastic. If you've only used a thin layer of paste, it will dry overnight on a nice summer's day or in a warm place in the house. Peel off the objects or bubble wrap before the paste dries out completely.

6. Next comes the printing. Prepare a big flat space on a large table and cover this with plastic and then a folded sheet to create a soft printing surface. Iron your fabric. Stretch your fabric out on top of the double-folded sheet and secure with pins onto the sheet. Have your bowl of Manutex paste and squeegee handy, ready to start printing.

7. Place the print screen on the fabric, pasted side down; spoon some of the Manutex paste into the frame, and use the squeegee to pull the paste through the screen. Your first prints will be quite hazy and light. As you continue to pull more paste through the screen, however, the dried-up dye will start to dissolve and, bit by bit, the dye will start to get wetter and the printed colours will intensify. Continue to turn the screen to create different patterns and print on top of the earlier, lighter sections.

8. It's difficult to know when to stop. But when you decide that you have finished printing, you can use a household spray filled with a strong soda solution to give the fabric an extra spray before rolling it in a sheet of plastic, long enough to cover the whole piece. The roll needs to be left to cure in a warm place for at least 24 hours – preferably longer.

9. Finally, you can unwrap the fabric, give it a good rinse and wash it, using a gentle non-bleach detergent, before leaving it to dry and then ironing it. And admire!

After three attempts, I finished up with a piece of cloth that would be perfect for my mother-of-the-bride dress. The graphic lines of the sides of the screen showed on the first two pieces. To avoid this happening again, I curved my squeegee movement and gently swept the paste around the larger of my screens in order to achieve a softer pattern.

Despite its unwanted lines, I loved the first printed piece, so I decided to make it up into a dress-shaped quilt. I backed it with wadding and quilted the dress very freely, adding beads and circles of dyed, stitched and cut-away silk organza to give some extra texture. I carried this with me for several months so I could add stitches whenever I had a spare minute or two, often while travelling, and the happy colours attracted many appreciative comments from passers by. I soon discovered that I had to stop explaining how I printed the fabric, however, as I could see eyes starting to glaze over.

The finished dress-shaped quilt complete with a pretty covered coat-hanger and lavender bags, was a last-minute entry at the Festival of Quilts, where it managed to win a prize.

The dress itself I wore with pride on the day of my daughter's wedding and the florist made the perfect corsage to complement it. The quilt remains a beautiful reminder of what was an unforgettable day.

Right:

'Mother-of-the-Bride'
Prizewinning quilt made of linen
fabric printed with a dissolving silk
screen, quilted with a combination
of hand and machine stitching and
embellished with beads and silk
organza spirals.

3 LUTRADUR LANDSCAPES AND BOXES

Lutradur is a non-woven polyester. The raw material is melted and spun through narrow jets to form endless fibres that are stretched by hot air flows and laid into a web. One of its uses is as a backing for automotive carpets.

It is similar to Vilene, but has a slightly crisper feel, and comes in a variety of weights, ranging from 30 to 120. It is also available in a range of colours, but I prefer to use the white or black version and apply my own colour. Lutradur is a very strong fabric and is very hard to tear. When cut, it doesn't fray, which makes it suitable for making many kinds of 3-D items, such as boxes, bags and book-wraps. Due to its crispness, it can easily be fed through most of the home-office printers without any additional backing. Its possibilities are endless. I will try and cover as many of them as possible, but through 'what-if' experiments ('what if I do this' or 'what if I try that'), my students, other textile artists and I keep coming up with new and exciting ways of using Lutradur.

Above:
From left to right: Lutradur 30 is thin and quite transparent and when painted it is suitable for appliqué as tree tops or wispy clouds; Lutradur 70 white is my preferred weight. Still slightly transparent, it is firm enough to stitch by machine or hand; Lutradur 70 black works well when painted with gold, silver and pearlescent acrylic paints.

Above:
Box made from painted, printed
and stitched (70 weight) Lutradur
(see pages 58–63 for box
construction).

Colouring Lutradur

Lutradur can be coloured in much the same way that you would dye fabric, but with the advantage that you won't need to wash it first, and there is no soaking in soda or other chemicals, no rinsing, washing or ironing. All you have to do is just paint it and leave it to dry and it's ready to use. If you use a fairly diluted paint, you will find that the fibres carry the paint colours into each other in fascinating ways, running into each other to create beautiful and unpredictable patterns, which in turn might inspire something completely different from your original concept.

The most easily available paint with which to colour Lutradur is acrylic paint. Acrylics come in a wide variety of colours and tubes can often be purchased at very reasonable prices at discount stationery stores.

Other suitable paints include fabric paints, Setacolor, watercolours (although you will only get very pale colours with these), acrylic inks, Koh-i-noor water-based dyes, emulsion paints and Markal oil sticks. Because Lutradur is 100 per cent polyester, transfer paints work very well. You can also use procion dyes, although I have found that because Lutradur is synthetic and procion dyes are mainly used for natural fabrics, they leave only very faint colours when painted onto Lutradur and left to dry.

Lutradur landscape with Acrylic Paint

1. Before you start, you must cover your workspace and the surrounding area with plastic sheeting. Put an apron on and wear a pair of rubber gloves. You will be spraying the paint, so it gets just about everywhere!

2. The paints with which I most enjoy working are the acrylics. To get a soft wash of acrylic colour, take an old jam jar, put in a tablespoon of paint and two or three tablespoons of water, depending on the strength of colour desired, and then mix it with a plastic fork or spoon. I have tried buying all kinds of plastic spray bottles, some with a pump action, only to find they clogged up after just one use. Since watching American fibre artist Barbara Lee Smith's DVD, I've taken a leaf out of her book and gone back to basics, using jam jars and the cleaned, working spray top of a used-up household spray.

Right:
Equipment for colouring Lutradur: acrylic paint, sponge, spray-top, brush and jam jar.

3. If you find spray painting too messy and wet, another very easy way of applying paint is to use a sponge. An ordinary soft, thin kitchen sponge, dipped into slightly thinned-down acrylic paint on an old plate, offers a slightly more controlled way of getting colour onto your sheet of Lutradur. You can still get the colours to blend into each other by spraying your piece with plain water in some areas, which makes the paint a bit wetter so the colours run.

4. It is best to start with the 'wettest' process first, as this takes the longest time to dry. Even when thinned down, however, I find that acrylic paint dries quite quickly, especially if you leave the piece outside on a fine day.

5. First cut a couple of pieces of Lutradur, cutting them slightly bigger than the desired finished size of your work. I've suggested two pieces, because one often turns out better than the other, and it's a good idea to have an extra piece on which to try out your spray or colour before starting on your 'best' piece. The spare one can always be cut into strips to be appliquéd onto the original, or used as a piece on which to photocopy or it can become the background for another design.

Below:

'Reservoir Sailing'. A spray-painted background with appliquéd sun, sails and grasses with simple machine stitching.

6. If you are intending to make a landscape picture, you can create a horizon by using another piece as a resist: place this as a straight line where you would like your horizon to be and then spray the sky with a selection of blues. Close to the horizon, the sky is usually a light blue, becoming darker as you look upwards. This effect can easily be achieved by mixing three shades of blue and spraying them so they just touch and run into each other.

Alternatively, you can try spraying a very fine mist first before making it more solid as you move up. Leave the sky to dry for 10 minutes or so before moving on to spray the lower part of your landscape – in other words, your fields – as this will prevent the two colours running into each other.

7.   As fields are usually yellow or green, you will need to place a resist piece to cover your sky and then sponge or spray your fields or foreground.

8.   Sometimes, foreground colours will run into your sky or you might blob or spill some other colour on your background, but don't worry too much about this – pieces can be stuck on afterwards or the 'mistake' can be turned into a surprising design feature!

9.   If you are looking at a hilly horizon, you can cut your resist piece into a curvy line. Place the top half of the resist on the horizon and sponge or spray your hills onto your horizon. They can be accentuated later on with Markal oil sticks, as explained on page 52.

10. As you move your wet painted pieces of Lutradur from the plastic sheet, you will discover it has created interesting patterns on the plastic. If you place a sketchbook, a piece of plain paper or even a strip of white fabric on the paint and gently press it with a cloth or a rolling pin or bottle, you can make a mono-print.

11. You will need to dry the painted sheets on a plastic base, not paper, because acrylic paints will stick to paper as they dry.

12. Next, you can create a piece in more solid colours by painting it with a wet paintbrush and undiluted acrylic paint(s). This piece can either be cut up and the pieces used to add contrast to your main work or used as a piece on its own. Again, you can use the underlying paint to mono-print pages in your sketchbook or a spare piece of fabric.

13. If you cut up a sponge into squares or circles and dip these into very slightly diluted paint, you can print the shapes on a lightly sprayed background.

14. Black Lutradur can be painted with fluorescent paints. The so-called interference media, such as pearlescent paint, also work well. Adding some lustre powders to ordinary acrylics will make the black sparkle as well!

15. You can cut a template out of a piece of card and use undiluted acrylic paint to stencil patterns onto Lutradur.

16. After all this painting and colouring, it's time for a break, so make yourself a cup of tea or coffee and leave the Lutradur to dry. Perhaps you could take the dog for a stroll and find some inspiration while you walk, thinking about the next layer of print or embellishment you are going to apply.

17. Cut an A4-sized sheet out of a lightly painted piece of Lutradur and photocopy a map, some words (a poem?), a music score or a photograph. *Remember to paint before you print,* or the printing will run. A map that relates to the area of your landscape picture can be photocopied to add a subtle bit of interest. Once it is cut up, it won't be easily recognised as 'the map', but it brings in a personal touch and old maps often have some nice textured shading. You will have to choose a map with some definite black/white contrast if it is to show up on the background, as the fibres of the Lutradur will slightly dull the image.

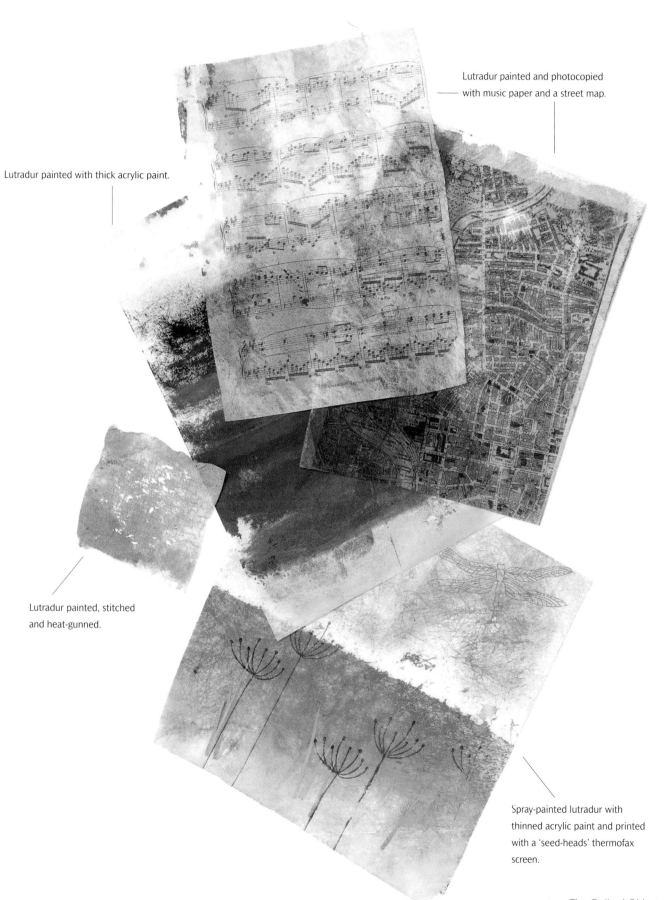

Lutradur painted and photocopied with music paper and a street map.

Lutradur painted with thick acrylic paint.

Lutradur painted, stitched and heat-gunned.

Spray-painted lutradur with thinned acrylic paint and printed with a 'seed-heads' thermofax screen.

Markal Sticks

These are oil sticks that can be painted or brushed onto fabric, paper or Lutradur. They are a good way of adding colour in a specific area, using a template, as the colours do not run like wet paints. I like to use a slightly curved template cut out of card and Markal sticks to paint some distant mountains or background grasses, as shown on the left.

Stamps

Sets of alphabet stamps are available now in all kinds of hobby and craft stores. They are ideal for adding free-form text to your piece or your sketchbook. You can use an ordinary stamp-pad with inks or paint some acrylics onto a piece of plastic and press into that. Just remember to clean the stamps afterwards!

Foil

Printer's foil comes in a wide range of colours and interesting patterns. It can be applied to Lutradur, fabric or paper, and you will find that little bits of glitter in the sky or on the water can make all the difference. To apply, use strips or shapes of Bondaweb and iron these onto the Lutradur. Leave the piece to cool and then peel off the paper backing. Next, place the foil, shiny side up, on the piece of Bondaweb. Cover this with baking parchment and iron with a medium iron. When it is cool, lift away the baking parchment and peel off the sheet of foil. You should be left with a nice piece of sparkle.

Another easy way of applying gold or silver is by backing foil sweet or chocolate wrappers. The plastic ones will melt, so you need to test them first. Try ripping them: the plastic ones won't rip, while the foils ones will. Back the foil wrappers with Bondaweb; cut small shapes out; peel off the backing paper, and iron to fix.

Above:
'Malvern Sunset'. Spray-painted Lutradur background with appliquéd hills and lines of darker painted Lutradur. Accents are applied with Markal oil sticks, and the glittery highlights come from printer foil and gold chocolate foil wrappers. It is machine quilted from the back.

Soldering Iron

Lutradur can be melted with a soldering iron or a heat gun. By cutting it with a soldering iron, you can create intricate shapes that would be difficult to achieve by cutting with scissors.

Safety Precaution

The melting fumes can be dangerous, so when using a soldering iron or heat gun, make sure your room is well ventilated and wear an appropriate respirator.

Heat Gun

Lutradur can be melted with a heat gun to create lovely organic and lacy shapes. Used on some pieces that are painted with green or brown acrylic, you will create good rocks and lichen type shapes.

Another interesting way of playing around is to paint the Lutradur and then free-machine it with an all-over pattern, using metallic thread (if you're not that confident with your free-machining, just stitch a straight grid pattern). The next stage is to heat-gun the piece. You will find that you have to hold the gun quite close to the material to melt it, so it's best to practise on a spare piece first. Brenda Boardman's piece below has been created using this method.

TIP
I apply Bondaweb to Lutradur before cutting out intricate shapes such as grass, trees and damselflies. The backing paper comes off quite easily and they can be fixed onto the background with an iron. Bits and pieces can also be stuck on with 505 spray glue.

Left:
Lutradur stitched in lacy patterns, melted with a heat gun and embellished with buttons and lace. By Brenda Boardman..

Right:
Black Lutradur heavily stitched, melted and embellished with gold foil and red ribbon. By Brenda Boardman.

Experimentation

Many artists really enjoy experimenting with the Lutradur product and everyone seems to come up with something completely different, so ideas are often exchanged and taken further again. A local artist named Brenda Boardman has explored Lutradur extensively and has come up with some brilliant pieces.

As Lutradur is very heat tolerant, it lends itself extremely well as a fabric for lampshades, as you can see with these very simple square glass lantern style lights, covered with painted, stitched and heat-gunned pieces.

As mentioned before, printing with Thermofax screens gives you a unique fabric to work on. Through trial and error, I found out that areas that are printed with screenprinting inks do not melt under the heat gun, giving us the opportunity to create lace patterns using a Thermofax screen and ink.

Right and left:
Lampshades built up of
double layers of heavily
machined Lutradur and
melted with a heat gun. By
Brenda Boardman.

Creative Lutradur

When all the sprayed and painted Lutradur is dry, you can start creating. This is an ideal medium for making smaller landscape pictures or postcards or for trying out a design on a small scale before embarking on the bigger quilt.

1. The landscapes are built up of layers. You've painted the background and can now start putting in the details by backing the smaller pieces of painted Lutradur with Bondaweb and then cutting them into thin strips to make fields, trees, grasses, houses, boats, hills and so on. After cutting the shapes, peel off the backing paper and iron the bits and pieces into place. It is advisable not to have the iron too hot as it will distort the Lutradur slightly: I would suggest that you use a medium temperature, hot enough to melt the Bondaweb, but not so hot as to distort the Lutradur. Again, try it out first, as each iron is different.

2. When you're more or less happy with the result, stick another layer of Lutradur (or iron-on Vilene) onto the back to give it a bit more body before you start to stitch, by machine or by hand. Lutradur is surprisingly easy to hand stitch. Choose a thread that blends in well with the picture. You can either stitch from the front, so you can see where you're going, or use a decorative thread in your bobbin and machine stitch from the back. I find that the cheap Natesh threads work well in the bobbin, when stitching from the back, or you might like to use the bobbin as your thread-reel. Stitch in straight lines or free-machine an all-over pattern.

3. To finish, cut and/or seal the edges with a soldering iron and either mount on yet another one or two layers of Lutradur, using Bondaweb, or simply mount your finished piece on a piece of watercolour paper.

Above:
Lutradur is an ideal medium for design experimentaton. This small A4 piece was made into the large 'Sunset' quilt shown on page 34.

Right:
A selection of A4 journal quilts all made with Lutradur.

Project: a Dragonfly Box

As Lutradur does not fray and can be fused with Bondaweb, I have discovered that it's an ideal medium with which to make little boxes and other origami-based objects. Card-making and craft shops often have books of origami patterns, which can be an excellent source of inspiration. In one of my workshops, a student showed me a dragonfly she had made using layers of sheer fabrics, which immediately sparked a creative 'what-if' thought process.

As soon as I had some spare time, I played around and found a way to create little creatures and other shapes out of Lutradur and organza, teaming this idea up with another one which had been floating in my head for a while: to make little boxes. This project describes how to make one of the little boxes, complete with a dragonfly or butterfly.

Below:

Sketchbook pages showing designs for the dragonfly box.

Left and above:
Lutradur boxes with butterfly and dragonfly designs.

Materials and Equipment

For a box measuring approximately 9 cm (3¼ in) each way, you will need to cut the following:
- Painted Lutradur (I used the 70 weight) – one 24 cm (9½ in) square and one 23 cm (9 in) square
- Bondaweb – 8 strips, each measuring approximately 4 x 5 cm (1½ in x 2 in)
- Several scraps of polyester sheer organza, each about 13 cm (5 in) square

You will also need a fine-tipped soldering iron to cut the butterfly or dragonfly for the top (alternatively, you can cut this with sharp scissors, but you will still need a soldering iron to burn out the small holes in the wings).

To familiarise yourself with folding the box, I suggest you try one out with a paper square first (see also diagram on page 62).
- First fold along all the dashed lines next to diagonal shading, as shown in figure 1.
- Next, cut along the solid lines, marked with arrows.
- Fold opposite corners B and D towards the centre.
- Fold the little flaps as shown in figure 2 towards each other at opposite ends to make a box shape.
- Fold ends A and C over these flaps to meet in the centre point.
- Sharpen the folds with your fingernails.

1. To make the box out of Lutradur, first cut the two squares, as mentioned above, out of painted Lutradur.

2. The dragonflies can be printed on the larger square with a computer printer, a stamp or a Thermofax screen, which is the method I used (there is more about Thermofax screens further on in this chapter).

3. Before starting to fold the box shape, you need to free-machine embroider the butterfly or dragonfly, using an attractive variegated and/or metallic cotton or polycotton thread.

4. To make the butterfly or dragonfly for the top, start by layering a separate piece of Lutradur, with a printed image on it, with three pieces of the sheer polyester organza (do not use silk, as this cannot be burned away with a soldering iron).

5. With a variegated and/or metallic thread in the top and the bobbin, drop the feed dogs of your sewing machine and free-machine along all the lines in one continuous stitch line, going over the outside lines twice. You might like to use a variegated or plain thread first and then highlight certain areas with a metallic or glitter thread afterwards.

6. You can now heat up your soldering iron. You will need to work on a heatproof base, such as a metal baking sheet or piece of marble or glass. Remember to wear a respirator and work in a well-ventilated area.

7. Gently run the tip of your soldering iron along the outside lines of the butterfly or dragonfly, separating the wings if possible. Prick out little dots or draw out areas within the wings to create a translucent effect.

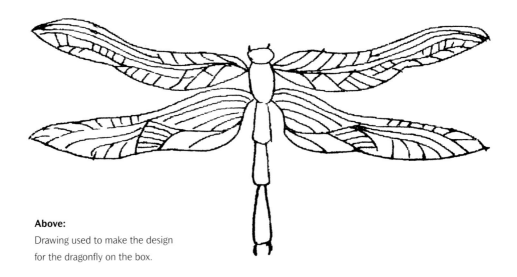

Above:
Drawing used to make the design for the dragonfly on the box.

Below:
The dragonfly outline was stitched onto layers of polyester organza and Lutradur, before being cut with a soldering iron.

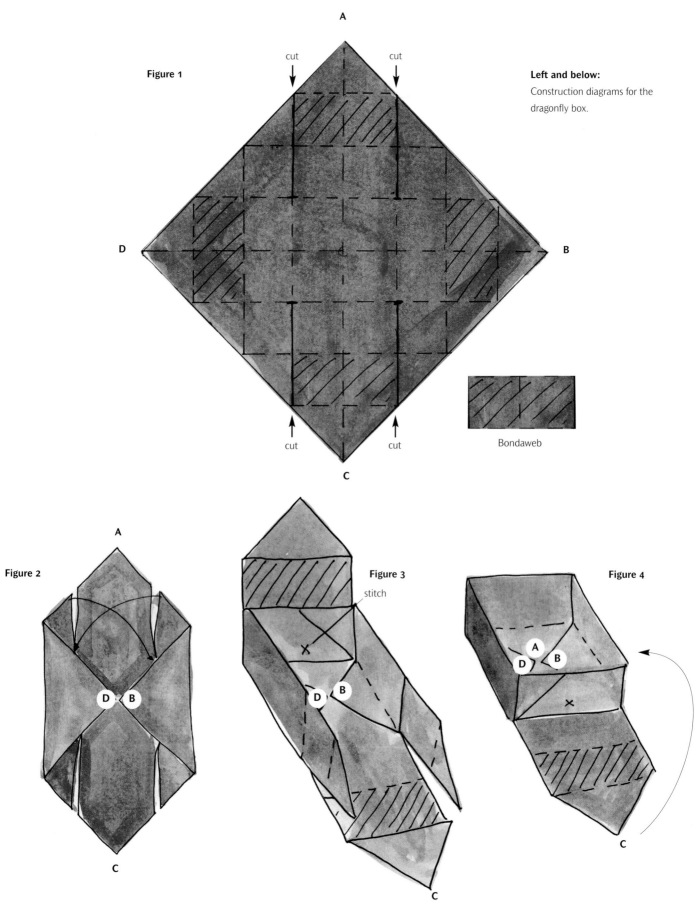

Figure 1

cut   cut

A

D   B

cut   cut

C

Left and below:
Construction diagrams for the dragonfly box.

Bondaweb

Figure 2

A

D   B

C

Figure 3

stitch

D   B

C

Figure 4

A
D   B

C

Above:

The construction stage for the
dragonfly box, just before the box is
folded into shape at stage 13:
motifs are stitched on, side flaps
are folded and other fold lines are
marked with stitching.

8. Now return to the box. Before you stitch the dragonfly in place, it is advisable to fold the box in order to mark the lines so you will know where to place it.

9. Continue folding the Lutradur squares. Fold along all the dotted lines, as on figure 1, and then cut along the solid lines, marked with arrows.

10. Iron a strip of Bondaweb to each of the areas marked with hatching.

11. Peel the paper off the Bondaweb on folds D and B, press them towards the centre and then iron the folds.

12. Straight stitch (feed dogs up) in one line along the folding lines, as shown in Figure 3, with the same thread as you used for your embroidery (this sharpens the folds), starting with a few stitches on the spot to anchor the thread. If there is butterfly on one of these lines, start and finish there (hiding any loose ends).

13. Attach the dragonfly to the larger square, which will be the box lid, by stitching along the length of its body. Place it near an edge to give it that 'just landed' impression.

14. Now repeat the process with the side flaps (A and C), to form the box lid, and secure the edges together with a couple of stitches, by hand or machine.

15. Repeat the process with the smaller square to complete the box.

Inspiration for other boxes can come from nature and the seasons. To represent the autumn, beautiful leaves with stitching along the veins can be added to boxes, cards or quilts. The intricate patterns of snowflakes can be printed, stitched and cut out with a soldering iron. Christmas, of course, offers endless design possibilities, while the dragonfly method can be used to create spring tulips or other flowers.

Printing

As mentioned before, Lutradur will go through most printers without a support backing, so you can scan or simply photocopy your drawing onto the sheet of Lutradur. Stamping can also be used to transfer patterns onto Lutradur.

A relatively new way of screenprinting your patterns onto paper, fabric or Lutradur is by using a Thermofax screen. Thermofax screens can be made from anything you have drawn or printed that can be photocopied in black and white. A special thermal imager machine makes the thermofax screen (see suppliers on page 126). It transfers your image onto a mesh by burning away the black lines and areas. This mesh is then put into a frame and is ready for printing with a water-based screenprinting ink or thickened dye and a squeegee.

With care, Thermofax screens can be used over and over again. Even if the mesh gets damaged, it can easily be taken out and replaced. This printing method can give you hours of fun and many lengths of uniquely-printed fabric or Lutradur, or papers that can be turned into wrapping paper.

Below:

Thermofax screen and squeegee where the image of the dragonfly can be seen (see pages 58–63).

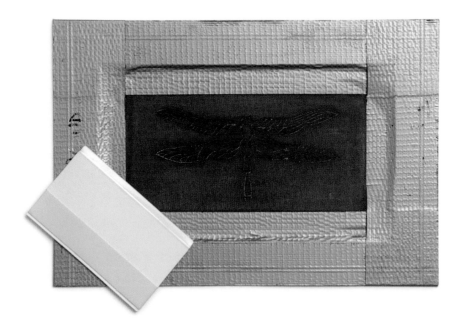

Right:
Hand-dyed and screen-printed
pieces of linen fabric, stretched and
stapled around a box canvas.

Designs in Lutradur with Barbara Lee Smith

I discovered Lutrador at the Knitting and Stitching Show in the UK through the work of the American fibre artist Barbara Lee Smith. Barbara was inspired by attending a workshop given by the British embroiderer Constance Howard, way back in 1973. Constance was the Principal Lecturer in Textiles at Goldsmiths College, London. Barbara loved her work and remembers Constance as someone who 'made everyone think a bit harder'. If you ever happen to come across a Constance Howard book, do buy it: they are invaluable when you are stuck for a stitch! The *Constance Howard Book of Stitches* is one of my favourite stitch inspirations and although it was published back in 1979, by Batsford, it still is a very contemporary book and full of ideas.

Barbara's large panels are based on the land and seascapes she encounters around the world, but the view that most inspires her the one from her studio on Raft Island, looking out over Puget Sound in the Pacific North West of the United States.

Her studio is a light, airy and almost spiritual place, with windows looking out over the ever-changing vistas of sky, sea and shifting tides. Inspiration on the doorstep! In fact, it amazes me how she gets any work done, as I would just sit and stare; which is exactly how Barbara's creative process starts. Her favourite quote is by Bernard Berenson:

> You must look, and look, and look … until you are blind with looking. And out of blindness comes illumination.

Combining all this inspiration with the fibrous material Lutradur, together with her paints and threads, she is able to create an atmosphere in her work that is like walking straight into weather. There are no frames to limit the vision, no hems to confine the energy that her work exudes. They are paintings, with added texture through stitching.

Barbara visited Giverny in France to catch the morning light in Monet's garden and the way she uses her collage technique is reminiscent of Matisse.

She starts her canvasses by painting sheets of Lutradur with thinned-down acrylics or fabric paints and the way the fibres carry the paints into each other can form the beginning of another masterpiece. In effect, she lets the fibres and paints do the talking. Next, from her library of coloured sheets, she cuts shapes, which are then pinned onto the background before being fused into place. Now it's time for the sewing machine to bind all these layers together with a web of flowing free-machine stitching in subtle colours. Her lines resemble topographical maps and show gentle undulating landscapes.

Layering is central to the way Barbara works: it's what makes each piece a quilt, but it also helps to build up the layers of the landscape. The background comes first, then the distance, followed by the nearest features.

Right:
'Landscape in Lutradur' by Barbara
Lee Smith, mounted on a double
layer of sprayed Lutradur.

4 POSTCARDS AND WALLHANGINGS

Among the most popular projects I have taught are the postcards. Whenever I teach making these as a workshop, many of the students are surprised to discover how little time, effort and material it takes to create one of these miniature works of art. One lady told me after a class that this was the only creative activity she could cope with and one of the few things that could take her mind off her treatment for cancer. Due to comments like this, I keep experimenting and, combining these efforts with an extremely topical passion for recycling, I've started looking around the house to find materials that could be used to make a postcard.

If you start by creating something small, such as a postcard, from materials that you've got at hand, you may find that this can be the stepping stone to a major and more meaningful project.

Postcards are fun to make and it's even better to be at the receiving end of one. In my studio, on the table behind my sewing machine, I have a container where I put all those off-cuts from whatever I am working on at the time that are a reasonable size. These bits are ideal for creating a quick mini-piece of textile art. But it does not always have to be a piece of fabric: anything that catches your eye can be incorporated in a 15 x 10 cm (6 x 4 in) postcard or the even smaller ATCs (Artist's Trading Cards), which are very popular in the United States. ATCs are mini pieces of art measuring 6 x 9 cm (2½ x 3½ in) and are traded or exchanged through websites. Many books and magazines are dedicated to these cards and by all accounts exchanging them can become quite addictive. This is a perfect way of trying out a new technique or using up bits and pieces left over from a major project.

The Exchange Challenge

We are all blessed with more materials than we could possibly need, so why not arrange a little exchange project with a friend or a group of textile enthusiasts? Brenda Boardman ran this challenge with her class and these were the rules:

First, find a postcard – an arty one or perhaps a landscape – and then fill a bag with bits of fabric, beads, ribbons and other found objects. Trade all these with a friend and challenge one another to make an A4 piece, based on the postcard and using the pieces out of the bag. Remember to set a deadline to have it completed by the next time you meet, so you can hand the finished project back to the person who gave it to you.

Materials

Anything that can be stitched or secured in an imaginative way can be used to make a postcard or fill a page in your sketchbook. The bits and pieces that you've collected over the years or have found on walks through the woods or on the beach have finally found a use!

Stamps from faraway places, buttons out of a button-box or cut from an old shirt, shells, old keys, the thin hanging ribbons they put in the new clothes you buy, dried flowers, raffia used to tie a beautiful bouquet, feathers, paint colour charts, the entry ticket to a memorable show or exhibition… The list is endless and so are the possibilities.

Right:
A selection of postcards and a
couple of the smaller Artist's
Trading Cards (ATCs).

Christmas Cards

Throughout the year there are so many occasions and celebrations that call for a handmade card, for example Christmas, birthdays, anniversaries, or just a card to say 'thank you'.

Sometimes, the easiest way to make your own personal cards in larger quantities, for occasions such as Christmas, is to make just one card and have it colour-copied onto A4 card. If you sit down with a pile of Christmas fabrics, Bondaweb and some threads and a good selection of favourite Christmas cards from previous years for extra inspiration, this can easily result in a few cards that can either be sent or used as designs for printed cards.

Above:
Strips of Christmas fabrics are fused and hand stitched onto a
postcard-sized piece of wadding. The dove motif is then added
by using Bondaweb and finished off with simple stitches.

Right:
Bauble shapes are cut out of silver fabrics and ribbon, then fused and stitched onto a co-ordinating background. Mirrors and beads are added to finish it off.

Below:
Little houses, domes and towers are cut out of Christmas-themed fabrics and backed with Bondaweb, hand-stitched and finished off with a machine around the edges.

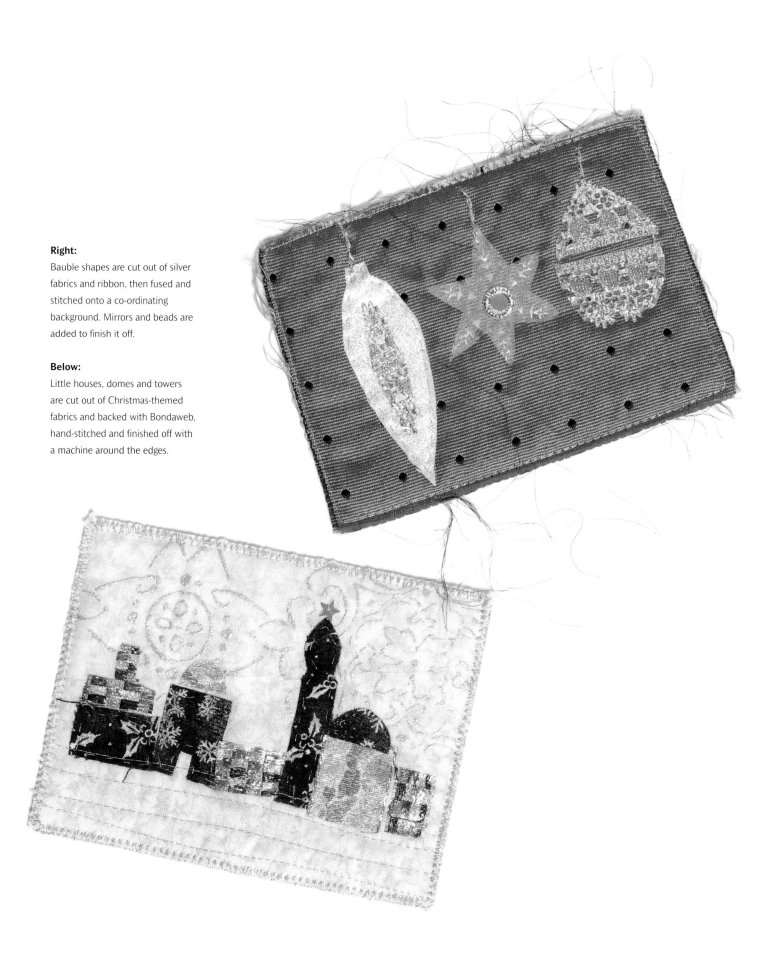

One particular Christmas card I loved so much that I decided to make it into a 37.5 cm (15 in) wallhanging. The simple shapes of the three kings were easily enlarged and traced onto Bondaweb. Next, picking them out of a basket full of fabrics in rich colours and textures, I selected several blues with gold and silver accents to make up the robes. I machine stitched them with straight and satin stitches and then started to decorate them with layers of net, lengths of braid, sequins, shisha mirrors and tassels. Each king seemed to take on his very own personality: a silver one, a gold one and another silver one. Gifts were made up, an individual crown was cut for each and their beards were glued in place. The background was quilted with simple lines and, of course, a guiding star in the sky, surrounded by little star-shaped sequins.

My first card was made in blues, but any combination of colours would work. Reds and gold on black is very mysterious, while vivid emerald green, ruby red and turquoise also works well.

repeat x 3

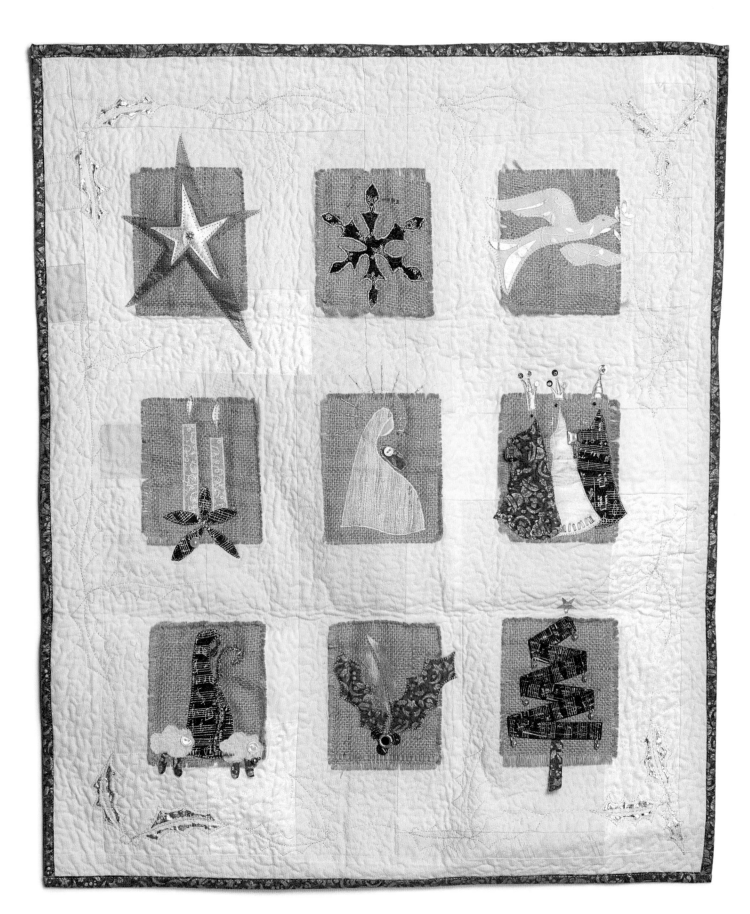

The year after that, I was inspired by a wallhanging made by Edwina Mackinnon, which combined several figures and shapes that relate to Christmas. The background was pieced and quilted first, and then postcard-sized pieces of hessian were stitched on. Finally, the various Christmas shapes were put in place on the wallhanging with Bondaweb and secured by stitching with a suitable thread.

My version of this hanging is made up of different whites, natural colours and hessian, with hints of gold to give a more subdued effect. The inspiration for the images came from my collection of favourite Christmas cards. Shapes were drawn or copied, traced in a mirror image onto Bondaweb and then fused onto the postcard rectangles.

Left:
Christmas wallhanging. Hessian rectangles are appliquéd onto a pieced and quilted cream background and decorated with designs inspired by a collection of Christmas cards

Right:
Details from the Christmas wallhanging.

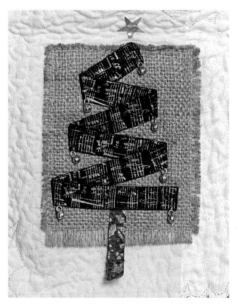

The finished product.

Pucked silk and
hand dyed cottons
constructed in four
pieces. Machine
and hand quilted.

Above:

Beautifully painted pages out of
Judith Hill's sketchbook, which
were used for the design of her
quilt on the right.

Right:

'Sunrise over Ben More Coigach'. Judith Hill's
wallhanging in four pieces is made with hand-
dyed cotton, linen, silk and satin fabrics. It is
quilted by hand and machine.

A Birthday Card

These cup cake birthday cards were quick and easy to make. The first thing you need is a good base to work on. If you are sewing the card by hand, it is best to start with a piece of wadding. I like to use the 80/20 fusible Hobbs Heirloom wadding because you can iron your fabrics onto it, secure it by hand or machine, and then continue to embellish it.

Start with a 10 x 15 cm (4 x 6 in) piece of white fabric placed on a piece of wadding of the same size. Repeat to create two fabric cards. On the first card, I appliquéd the paper cake cup and cake with Bondaweb, added some matching quilting, introduced a 'Happy Birthday' label and stitched the button on the top. On the second fabric card, I used a mini birthday cake image stamp on the fabric, stitched the contours of the stamp image and added the label. They were both backed with a 10 x 15 cm (4 x 6 in) rectangle of white fabric neatly straightened with a rotary cutter and ruler. The edges were finished off with coloured satin stitching to match the colour of the cake.

It's fun to work intuitively. If you are stuck for inspiration, pick up a good home or country magazine and leaf through it, ripping out bits and pieces that catch your eye. Alternatively, set yourself a challenge: just take eight or so scraps of fabric and see what you can do with those.

If you are taking a landscape picture as your inspiration, you should consider the colour first – but try not to use more than eight pieces, preferably in different shades or hues of one or two colours. This is only a small piece and too many colours can confuse the eye. If your landscape consists mainly of blues and greens, stick with those and add just one contrast.

Place your fabrics on the wadding and pin, spray-glue or iron them in place. You can then stitch by hand or machine to secure the pieces.

Opposite:
Cup cake birthday cards appliquéd with simple shapes and decorations.

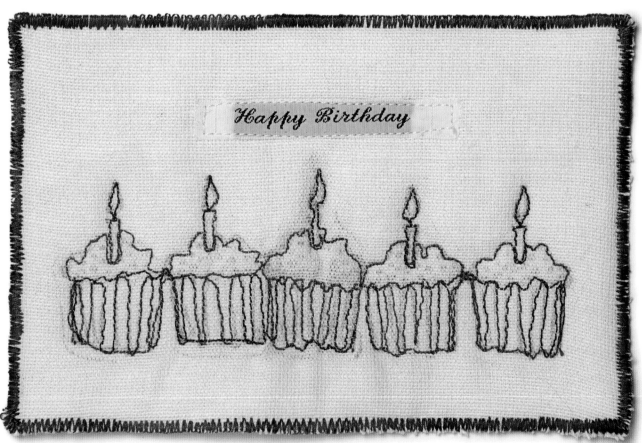

Project: Tulip Cards

1. I made a set of about six tulip cards to send to my friends. I started off with a larger – 32.5 cm (13 in) square – piece of fabric, which I ironed onto fusible wadding. Next, I machine quilted it with a simple wavy grid pattern to secure the three layers together and create a background pattern. I then found some fairly thick thread in a colour that coordinated well with the fabric and quilted this on, with the machine set to a narrow zigzag. I also found some scrim to add a bit of texture and stitched this on as well.

2. The quilted piece was then cut into 10 x 15 cm (4 x 6 in) postcard-sized pieces, on each of which I quilted a stem cut from ribbon or thin strips of felt.

3. To make the tulip heads, I started by ironing Bondaweb onto pieces cut from a range of red fabrics and then cut out lots of simple tulip-petal shapes.

4. After peeling away the backing paper, I arranged three or four of these petals to make up each tulip and ironed them to fix them in place, finishing with a bit of free-machine quilting.

5. Text can be added by printing suitable wording onto fabric with the computer printer or with a stamp and then stitching over the wording afterwards. If you want a more professional finish, perhaps because you are intending to make cards on a more regular basis, you can order your own woven textile labels, saying 'Thank You', 'Happy Birthday' or 'Congratulations', from a school name-tag supplier.

6. To make the backing for cards of this type, I like to iron some more Bondaweb onto a piece of calico, in order to give it some firmness, and cut this again into 10 x 15 cm (4 x 6 in) rectangles. I then draw the postcard address lines onto the back of each of them and iron them to fix.

7. Cut the edges neatly with scissors or a rotary cutter and then finish with a satin stitch or an ordinary straight stitch and stitch around the outside a couple of times, keeping close to the edge.

Far right
Step 1: A layer of wadding and dyed fabric, quilted and decorated with threads and ribbon.

Right:
Step 2: Cut into six postcard-sized rectangles.

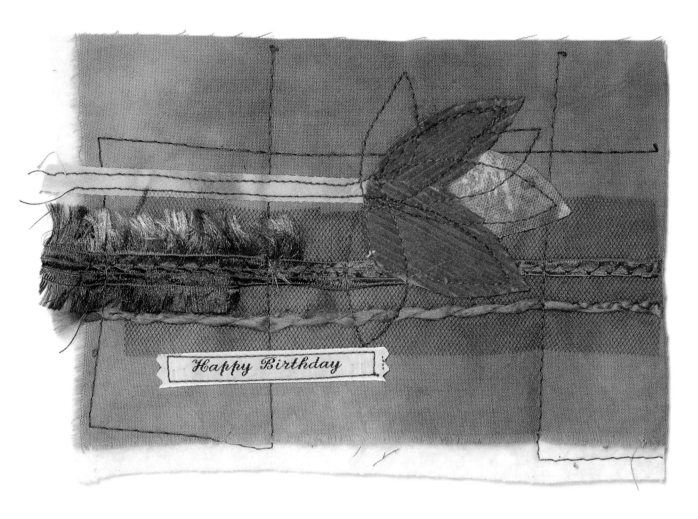

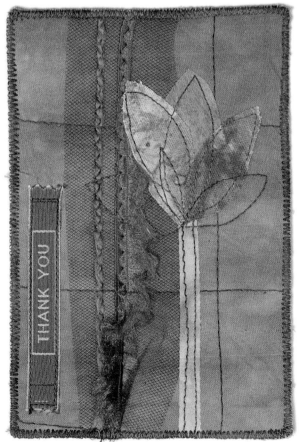

Step 3: A stem, petals and a message is
stitched on each card separately.

Step 4: The backing is fused on, the edges
trimmed and the card finished with a colourful
satin stitch.

Jenny Rolfe's Mini Quilts on Box Canvas

Jenny is a British quilter who, after making more quilts than she could find beds to put them on, decided to down-size and concentrate on making smaller hangings, bags and purses, with an emphasis on embroidery. Jenny and I shared a stand at the Festival of Quilts in the UK for a couple of years and, at the end of each show, we exchanged our demonstration projects.

Jenny makes her mini-quilts to match the size of ready-made box canvases that are used for painting. To make this piece, she ironed Bondaweb onto a square of pelmet Vilene and then placed small squares and rectangles of left-over fabrics, all in shades of one particular colour, to cover the Vilene base. To fuse them into place she ironed it with a sheet of baking parchment between the iron and the work (this protects the fabric). She then placed a square of fine tulle over the piece and pinned it to hold the layers together. Using matching variegated thread she decorated the piece with lots of machine stitching in a simple geometric pattern.

Right:

An embroidered seed head on a background of mixed squares, mounted on a box canvas by Jenny Rolfe.

Next, Jenny free-machined a pattern inspired by the beautiful seed heads of cow parsley, this time in a contrasting thread. The piece was then cut to exactly the same size as the ready-made canvas squares. The edges were machined with a very tight zigzag and the finished piece was applied to the canvas square with PVA glue.

Seeing Jenny work with these little canvases immediately sparked my own imagination. As a lot of my work is based on landscapes, this was an ideal possibility to display small pieces of work of this nature. So instead of making a 10 x 15 cm (4 x 6 in) postcard, I made a 12.5 cm (5 in) square in exactly the same way as a postcard, finished it with a satin-stitch and glued it to the canvas (see pages 84 and 85).

So many ideas and materials are available nowadays, but the simple ones are often the best.

Right:
Tulip on a box canvas made using Jenny Rolfe's technique.

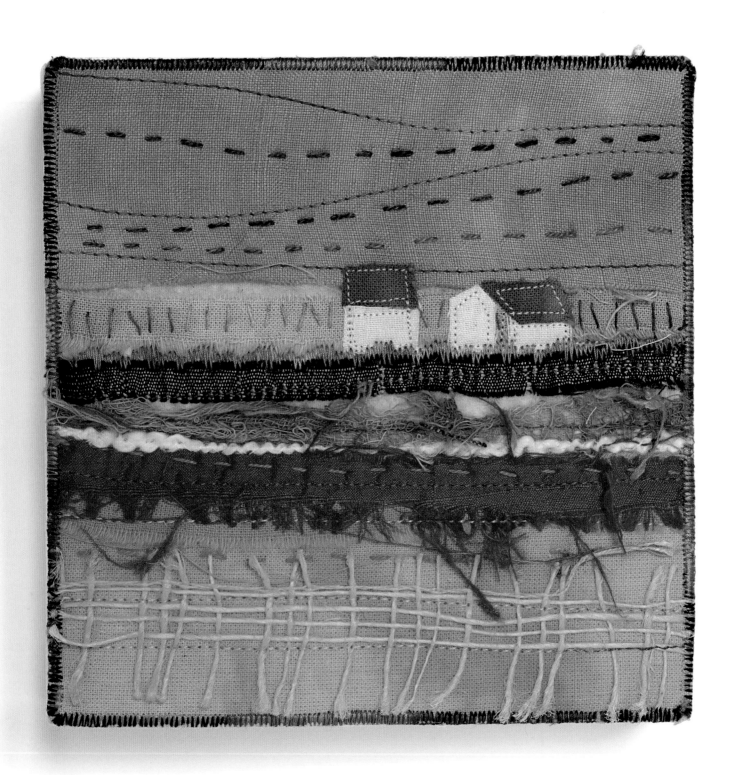

Project: Mini-quilt Mounted on a Canvas Box

1. To make a 12.5 cm (5 in) square postcard and mount it on a chunky canvas box, start with a base of about 14 cm (5½ in) square: this could be a piece of medium-weight calico, covered with Bondaweb or heavy (iron-on) interfacing.

2. Choose your design – I used a picture as my inspiration – and then, taking fabrics from your scrap bag, cut several strips, each about 14 cm (5½ in) long, and place them on the square, copying your inspiration picture.

3. Iron to fix them in place with the Bondaweb, and then machine stitch soft flowing lines in thread of a matching colour.

4. Next, add some pieces with interesting textures to the central element of your design (i.e. a house, trees, a boat or a fence), again using Bondaweb to hold them in place before machine stitching to secure them.

5. Now your mini landscape can be finished off with some hand and/or machine stitching in a contrasting colour of thread. This is a good time to have a look at the colour wheel if you can't decide what colour to use and take a colour that is the opposite to your background colour.

6. Now cut the finished piece to the exact size of your canvas box, and use your machine to satin stitch round the square a couple of times to give a good solid finished edge, using a coloured thread that blends in with the picture.

7. If you've worked on heavy Vilene, you can glue the square to the canvas box with a good coating of PVA and leave it to dry for 24 hours. If you have worked on calico, you will need to fuse it onto some Vilene before securing it to the box with PVA glue.

Left:
'Summer Landscape' mini quilt on a
12.5-cm (5-in) canvas box.

5 BAGS, PURSES AND THREE-DIMENSIONAL PROJECTS

Bags are among my favourite projects and I'm sure I'm not alone in this. They come in all sizes and shapes and you can employ all sorts of different techniques, so that each one turns out unique. And they are so useful, as well!

Many of my bags are inspired by landscapes, but of course the design on any of the bags featured here can be changed to incorporate your own favourite design source. More often than not, I have used old clothes or fabrics to make these bags, so in this era of recycling they are extremely 'green'.

The first bag I made for my City and Guilds course was a small rucksack. I had just learned the basics of free-machine quilting and found out what a walking foot was! Both of these techniques were used to quilt the bag, which was made of simple brown cotton. From those very early days, I often chose to include a piece of leather, especially on the base, to make it weatherproof. I went to the famous 'rag market' in the city of Birmingham, England and found an old pair of hot-pants, made of the softest brown nappa leather. The nappa was perfect and it stitched beautifully too!

The next bag was designed to carry my cutting mat and other accessories. The blocks were made from a variety of out-of-fashion checked shirts that had been discarded by my children. One of the first projects organised by my quilt group, 'The Marlbrook Quilters', was a 'block of the month' series. Each member took it in turns to choose a block, work out the instructions and show how it was constructed. Most of the blocks were turned into quilts, but I joined mine into two panels, large enough to house the cutting mat. The narrow side panels were made from left-over strips and two lengths of wooden dowling were inserted in the quilted loops at the top to make simple carrying handles.

Below:
Two bags made by folding a 30-cm (12-in) quilted and decorated square. The pink scissor bag is made by stitching two adjoining sides of a square together. The grey chenille bag, made by Linda Kemshall, has been folded and stitched like an envelope.

Right:

For those of you who prefer a bit more colour, I created this urban landscape bag from material in my scrap bag. It is based on the same pattern as on pages 91–93, but each house panel was made individually with the window and doors appliquéd on with Bondaweb.

Denim

Over the years, I have been unable to throw out some of the better-labelled denim jeans, even when they were worn out at the knees and hems. Instead, I secretly hoarded them under my work table, knowing that one day I would find the perfect use for them. The pile grew and every now and then I would experiment with bits and pieces, adding T-shirts as a lining, but the heavy weight of the denim made finished pieces just too heavy to be comfortable as quilts.

One fine day, several ideas just clicked together: I found the right shape of bag and married it to a seascape. All those different colours of denim – the dark ones that weren't the right fit, the medium-coloured ones with broken zips and the really pale blue washed and worn out frayed ones – provided me with the ideal colours to make a seascape in blue.

I started unpicking a few hems and seams, discovering the most fantastic markings where the fabric had been turned in and the garment had been washed and worn. Even the frayed downtrodden back-hems gave me lots of texture.

As always, my first step in any new project was to make something small. Postcards are the ideal stepping stone, so I started by placing small ripped strips on some fusible wadding or iron-on Vilene in a 'seascape' kind of way. Some simple straight machine stitching was added. Next a couple of sails, seagulls, sun or some beach huts were stuck on with a bit of Bondaweb (double-sided iron-on) and then stitched. Even these features were taken from the old jeans, being cut from the white inside pocket linings! A bit of old sheeting or a rectangle cut from an old shirt was stuck on the back, again with Bondaweb, and the postcard was ready to send and be received by a very happy recipient.

Project: Denim Bag

Materials

- 2 or 3 old pairs of jeans in a light, medium and dark denim
- 80 x 150 cm (32 x 59 in) wadding (I use Hobbs Heirloom 80/20 fusible)
- 80 x 150 cm (32 x 59 in) lining fabric

A similar design was used to make the large bag, featured here. I needed a bag big enough to carry and protect the small sewing machine that I take to workshops. Because the handles are an integral part of the structure, the bag is strong enough to carry quite a heavy load. To make the bag, I suggest you use three pairs of jeans in a range of colours: dark, medium and light. Remember the fabric has two sides, both of which can be used.

1. The first stage is to spend an evening unpicking seams and hems, revealing lovely textured bits of fabric. You need to do this because, if you try stitching through the thick side seams of a pair of jeans, you will break many needles and even the toughest sewing machine will struggle. I like to add a bit of white canvas or other white cotton fabric to create a nice contrast for waves and so on, and perhaps a house or beach hut. If you have a very soft piece of leather or an old suede jacket, you can use this for the base and the binding, with perhaps a house, tree or boat to carry the colour through.

2. The handles can be cut from the jeans legs. From the diagram, make and cut out a paper pattern for the handles to size and then cut the four handle pieces (seam allowances are included). To leave you a sufficient range of colours and add contrast and interest, I suggest you use one leg each of different jeans – perhaps two dark pieces and two light.

3. Leave some fabric for the base (it will measure approximately 37.5 x 30 cm/15 x 12 in). I usually leave cutting the base until I have put the back together and can check a more accurate size. You will need to cut one base out of denim or leather and one out of lining. You can cut the wadding later out of left-overs.

4. From a selection of different shades of denim, cut strips 80 cm (32 in) long, which is about the length of a leg, in widths ranging from 2.5 to 12.5 cm (1 to 5 in), using some unpicked hems and so on to add texture. If you cannot get long enough strips, just join two or three pieces to make up the required lengths or make two panels measuring 40 cm (16 in).

Below is a guide to colours used for the seascape:

White:	two 2.5 cm (1 in) strips
Light:	one 2.5 cm (1 in) strip and one 8 cm (3½ in) strip
Medium:	one 2.5 cm (1 in) strip and one 10 cm (4½ in) strip for sky
Dark:	one 6 cm (2½ in) strip for the bottom and one 7.5 cm (3 in) strip for the horizon

5. Lay these out to make a land- or seascape panel, about 36 cm (14¼ in) deep:

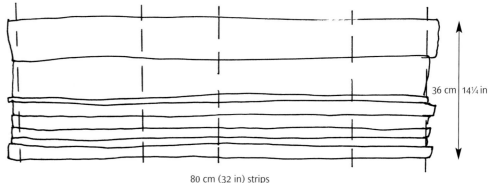

36 cm │ 14¼ in

80 cm (32 in) strips

Figure 1

- Start with a dark 6 cm (2½ in) strip at the base
- Next, add three or more narrower strips, in different shades; add a white strip for contrast and then have dark strip again for the horizon
- Above the horizon, take a light strip of 10 cm (4 in)
- Finish with a medium strip 10 cm (4 in) at the top

If the piecework goes banana shaped, don't worry. When you're cutting the panels, you can adjust each section as you go, but make sure the length allows for this!

6. Cut into four panels along the broken lines in figure 1. Make sure your strip is wide enough. If it is not, just the cut the panels narrower.

    Two x 23 cm (9 in) wide, for front and back
    Two x 16 cm (6½ in) wide, for sides.

7. Sew the handles and panel together as in figure 2.

8. Make your 'sandwich' for the bag and the base from the three elements: the stitched panel; a (fusible) wadding, and a backing fabric (old checked shirts are good for this). Tack or iron all three layers together. Don't cut the wadding and lining in between the handles yet. The layers might move whilst your quilting the bag.

9. Now you are ready to quilt. Keep the stitching simple – either straight lines, 2.5 or 5 cm (1 or 2 in) apart, or a grid of squares or diamonds. Keep 2.5 cm (1 in) on both sides free of stitching. This will help with the assembly. The wadding and the lining in between the handles can now be cut away close to the edge of the denim.

10. Now add boats, beach huts, sheep or farmhouses by ironing 10 cm (4 in) squares of Bondaweb on the back of some contrasting denim. Cut out required shapes (you can draw these on the paper backing of the Bondaweb); peel off the paper, and iron the shapes in place. Secure them with machine stitching. Now you can add some machine-embroidered pattern like the cow parsley.

11. You should also quilt the base. There's no need to keep the base sides free of stitching.

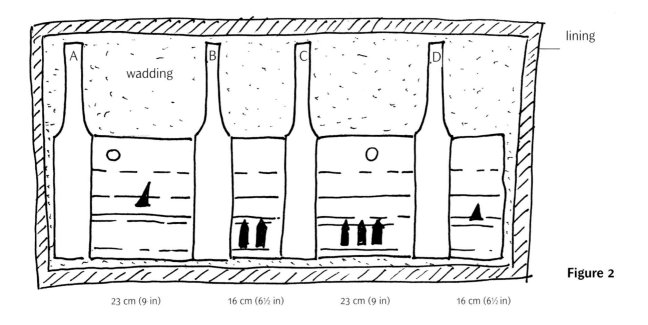

lining

wadding

A   B   C   D

Figure 2

23 cm (9 in)   16 cm (6½ in)   23 cm (9 in)   16 cm (6½ in)

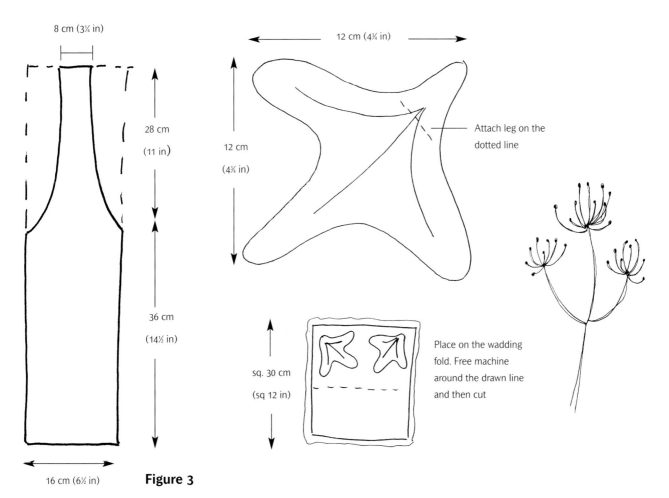

8 cm (3¼ in)

28 cm
(11 in)

36 cm
(14½ in)

16 cm (6½ in)   **Figure 3**

12 cm (4¾ in)

12 cm
(4¾ in)

Attach leg on the
dotted line

sq. 30 cm
(sq 12 in)

Place on the wadding
fold. Free machine
around the drawn line
and then cut

Assembly

12. In the side seams, cut back the wadding, leaving 1 cm (½ in) of the denim free. Pin only the denim into a 1 cm (½ in) side seam, right sides together, and machine stitch. Tuck the wadding under the seam allowance and then fold one side of the lining 6 mm (¼ in) under. Place over the other raw edge side of the lining, pin and hand stitch.

13. For the base layer, take a 37.5 x 30 cm (15 x 12 in) piece of denim or soft suede, and the same for wadding and lining fabric. Quilt in straight lines 2.5 cm (1 in) apart.

14. Pin the bag onto the base, matching the corners of the base with the centre of the bottom of each handle. Place the panels on the sides of the base. Stitch all around and finish the seam off with a satin stitch or some binding.

15. Attach handles A to D and B to C (see figure 2 on page 93) in the same way that you joined the side seams: cut back the wadding, and stitch right sides together first, then fold one side of the lining under and join the edges by hand or machine stitch.

16. To finish, cut 3 cm (1¼ in) binding strips out of a lighter denim (such as a shirt or skirt) or 2.5 cm (1 in) wide strips of leather. Join a sufficient length to go around the top edge of the bag. Stitch the strip on the inside of the bag; fold it over; turn the raw edge (if using fabric) under, and then pin and topstitch on the outside.

17. Pin and stitch on your label and enjoy your bag!

This bag pattern is very forgiving – it can easily be scaled down to make it smaller, I don't think you want it much bigger, because it will be much too heavy to carry.

Above:

Example of a landscape panel for a
recycled jeans bag.

Boxes, Bags and Altered Books

Angie Hughes is an embroiderer with an art studio in the beautiful town of Ledbury, in the heart of Herefordshire, UK, with its black-and-white half-timbered houses and narrow cobbled streets. Her work, inspired by the history and the landscape of this place, is versatile, with a distinctive style combining embellishments with heavy machine embroidery. Her signature is the use of letters and text on paper and fabric, printed with old original letter blocks borrowed from the friendly proprietor of the hand-set printing press shop down the road. Letters are not always formed into text and are sometimes used simply to add patterns.

Many of her pieces are inspired by poetry. She starts by making a base, dipping pieces of cotton interlining into a messy concoction of strong tea and PVA glue, squeezing them and then leaving them to dry. This turns the fabric into a heavy, ancient-looking textile that is a joy to stitch. After the fabric has been steam ironed, Angie layers pieces of scrim, tissue, lace and other interesting finds and then secures it all with machine embroidery. The result is then given a coat of gesso to seal it before it is coloured with thinned-down acrylic paints.

Angie's work is easily adapted to make smaller pieces, such as gorgeous brooches, cards and little framed pictures. She loves working and experimenting with rich materials, such as velvet, silks, felt, gold and silver foils, adding lots of stitching with bright sparkly threads. If ever I want to treat myself to a creative day out, I try and enrol on one of Angie's workshops.

Among her other projects are books. These may be 'altered' books, her own sumptuous sketchbooks or the covers that these books are wrapped up in, forming a complete package.

I took part in her altered book challenge, where we started with an old book bought at a market or second-hand book shop. Each book was divided into ten equal sections and every month the book was handed down to the next person on the list. It is very similar to the monthly journal quilt challenge. Pages could be painted, cut, ripped, embellished, printed or stuck down and stitched with whatever inspired you. At the end, all the books were returned to their rightful owners and displayed at an exhibition. As with the journal quilts, we found that being part of a circle makes you carry on because you do not want to break the chain, so you have to sit down each month and apply your creative mind to whatever is in front of you.

Below:

A richly embellished bag made at a workshop with Angie Hughes. It was inspired by the paintings of Gustav Klimt.

Project: Decorated Little Velvet Bags

One of Angie's most popular workshops involves making these gorgeous little bags and, having worked with Angie on a bag inspired by Klimt, I took the concept and found it adapted very well to a landscape design.

The bag design is based on the A4 pattern, figure 1 on page 98. The A4 pattern is traced onto iron-on interfacing and ironed onto the back of an A4 piece of dark velvet. I designed a simple Tuscan landscape and used it to cover all four sides of the bag. Houses, trees, paths and pebbles, cut from chocolate wrappers, printer's foil, velvet and sheers, are applied with a double-sided fusible web to a base of black velvet or felt. The whole piece is then covered with a polyester sheer fabric in a suitable colour and stitched with a variegated metallic and green thread. Thin lengths of cord are couched on with a narrow zigzag before the bag is stitched together and the lining is inserted. Ringlet holes are hammered in place and a cord is woven through and finished off with a handmade tassel.

My little bags usually hang from a door handle, where they can be admired by all visitors.

Below:

This is how the velvet bag looks before assembly.

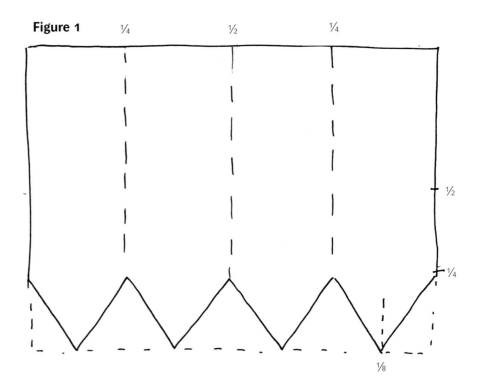

Figure 1

¼   ½   ¼

½

¼

⅛

A Decorated Box in Lutradur

The gift box on the right was made as a birthday present by my friend Sheila Nunnerly. It contained several reels of metallic threads, ready for me to start playing with. This I did the following week while trying to work out how the box was made.

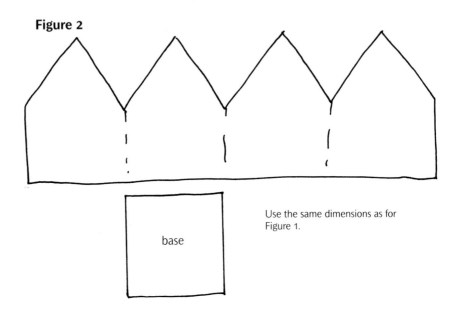

Figure 2

base

Use the same dimensions as for Figure 1.

1. Fuse together two A4 sheets of painted Lutradur with Bondaweb and cut out both shapes from figure 2; i.e. the box and a separate base of 7.5 cm (2⅞ in) square.

2. Embroider the edges with a decorative machine stitch in a metallic thread and decorate each centre with an appliqué shape.

3. With the same metallic thread and a length of string, the pretty cords were created by zigzag stitching over the string while gently moving backwards and forwards until it was covered with stitches.

4. This cord was then placed against the edge of the box and zigzagged onto the top edge around the top points and one side. The bottom edge and all around the square of the base was satinstitched with the same thread. The sides were zigzagged together and the base was stitched into place by hand. Equal lengths of decorated cords were attached to the top of each point and threaded through a big bead with a big hole, and the ends were finished off by folding a 2.5 cm (1 in) square of thin copper diagonally in half around the top of each cord.

Again, you can use your imagination to vary the size and the shape as you choose.

Right:
Embroidered gift box in Lutradur, based on a similar design as the velvet bags. Made by Sheila Nunnerley.

Dolls

I used plain calico and a Thermofax screen of one of my favourite poems to print the fabric to make this doll. The weekly class I go to, run by Edwina Mackinnon, used it as a challenge and the resulting collection of dolls proved an enormous success at our end-of-year exhibition.

The doll is made by folding 30 cm (12 in) of calico in half and drawing patterns for the body, head, arm and legs on to one side, leaving 2 cm (¾ in) allowance between each body part. Stitch along the lines of your drawings, leaving a gap at the top for stuffing. The eyes, nose and lips are drawn on with a fabric pen.

As speed is always the essence with me, I decided not to spend lots of time turning legs, arms and body inside out and left the raw edges showing, although I clipped the seams as close as possible.

All the body parts are then stuffed with a soft polyester fibre filling with the help of a crochet hook or something similar. The arms, legs and head are then stitched onto the body and a suitable hairdo can be created. The doll is then ready to be dressed.

With all those words on her body, I decided she was a poet and gave her a feather quill with which to write some more.

Left and right:
'She's a Poet' doll made with calico and printed with words from the poem 'Love Spell' by Kathleen Raine.

Project: Chicken

I love chickens and recently acquired a beautiful coop and some real hens that lay organic eggs. When I'm in my studio, I hear them clucking and scratching away. They have become good friends and enjoy being talked to. The three of them were the 'models' that inspired these pages in my sketchbook.

It was a natural progression to make 'one of my own' chickens out of fabric, so I delved into the big box of white fabric that stands in the corner of the studio.

Top:
My three hens: Ishy, Valerie and Wes.

Above:
Sketchbook pages filled with paintings, drawings, photos and collages of my three hens. They were the inspiration for the quilted chicken.

Right:
'Calico Chick'. Fun chicken made
out of frayed cottons and old lace.

Materials

- 50 cm (19½ in) of a medium-weight natural calico
- A small bag of fibrefill for the stuffing
- A 10 x 25 cm (4 x 10 in) strip of cotton wadding or cotton curtain interlining, for the legs
- A small bag of little stones or cat litter
- 50 cm (19½ in) of narrow elastic and some shearing elastic
- Small pieces of red and yellow felt, for beak and comb

Body

Cut two body sections out of calico. For the feathers, cut two 7.5 x 90 cm (3 x 36 in) strips of calico. Fold these down the full length of each strip and straight stitch ½ cm (⅛ in) from the fold line. Cut snips about 6 mm (¼ in) apart, cutting to about 1 cm (⅓ in) of the fold. Also make some feather strips to go around the ankle: cut two 6 x 50 cm (2½ x 20 in) strips; fold each in half; straight stitch close to the fold and snip as before.

Stitch three rows of feathers on each side of the body, starting below the neck, with each row overlapping the next by about half.

Legs

For the legs, cut a 12.5 x 37.5 cm (5 x 15 in) strip of calico and a strip of cotton wadding 6 cm x 37.5 cm (2½ x 15 in). Place the wadding on one side of the calico and fold in half lengthways to produce a sandwich with calico on the outer sides. Cut into two long strips each about 1.5 cm (¾ in) wide and discard the folded edge. Now stitch up and down the length about 10 or 12 times, with the lines of stitching set closely together.

Feet

Cut a 25 cm (10 in) square of calico and the same of wadding. Draw the two feet side by side on one half of the calico. Place the calico on the wadding; fold in half, and then free-machine (darning foot and feed dogs down) around the outlines of the feet two or three times and the inner lines. Cut out close to the stitching and then attach the legs towards the back of the feet.

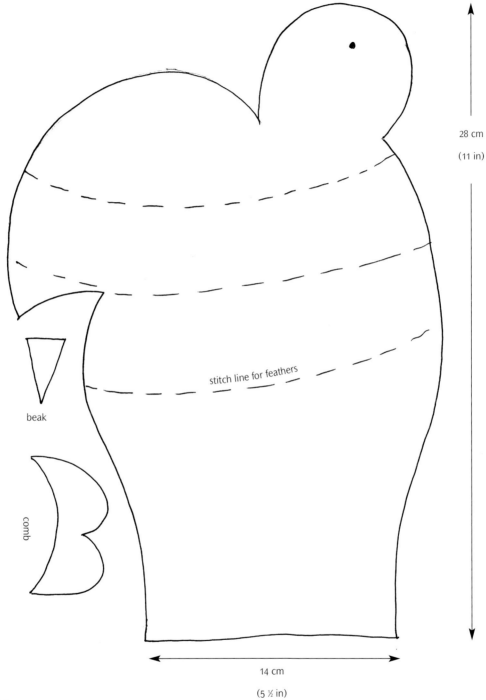

28 cm
(11 in)

stitch line for feathers

beak

comb

14 cm

(5 ½ in)

Figure

Body section for the chicken.

Tea Stain

Make a bowl of 200 ml (8 fl oz) of hot strong tea and soak the body and feet feathers for about 10 minutes. Squeeze out excess water and rub them dry in a towel or dry in the tumble dryer to fluff up the feathers. Next, add a generous tablespoon of PVA glue to the tea and soak the legs with the feet in this. Again, squeeze them and leave them to dry. The PVA will make them crispier.

Assembly

This depends on how you would like your chicken to look. For a neat finish, with the beak and comb facing in, stitch the body pieces with right sides together and then turn right side out. For the rough version, pin the beak and comb facing out and stitch with the wrong sides together, going round a couple of times to strengthen the stitching. For both versions leave the bottom open.

Insert fibrefill through the bottom, but leave enough space at the bottom to insert a small plastic bag filled with cat litter, small pebbles, rice or beans. This will help the chicken to sit up. Sew up the bottom by hand and stitch across the ends to give a flat finish.

With strong black thread, sew a black bead in position on one side of the head. Push the needle through the other side; pull the thread tightly, and sew the second bead to the other side.

When the legs are dry, trim them to 32.5 cm (13 in). Wind the narrow feathers round the ankle two or three times; cut away any left-over feather strip and hand stitch at the back. Now sew a leg to each side of the body.

Pants

Out of calico, cut a piece measuring 30 x 90 cm (12 x 36 in). With right sides together, sew the short sides together, finishing the seam with satin stitch if you choose. Still with right sides together, measure the centre and stitch an upside-down V in the centre about 15 cm (6 in) up from one edge. Cut in and finish the seam. Satin stitch the top end and fold a 12 mm (½ in) seam towards the inside. Stitch and thread narrow elastic through the fold; tighten it to size, and then sew the ends together and close the gap. By hand, straight-stitch some shearing elastic about 1 cm (½ in) through the bottom of each leg: pull tight and tie the ends together.

Apron

I used an old antimacassar for the apron on page 103, but another piece of calico trimmed with some pretty lace would look just as good. Cut a piece of calico measuring 36 cm x 10 cm (14 x 4 in); trim the sides and bottom with lace, and then gather the top. Cut a waistband measuring 70 x 7 cm (28 x 2½ in); sew the gathered apron to the middle of the waistband; taking a 6 mm (¼ in) seam allowance, stitch around the remainder of the waistband, wrong sides together. Turn out and press. Topstitch the other side of the waistband to the apron skirt. Make a bib by folding a 5 x 13 cm (2 x 5 in) piece of calico in half and stitching around, leave a gap for turning. Clip the corners and turn it out. Stitch it to the middle of the apron and attach lengths of ribbon as ties.

You can now dress your chicken!

Sheep

The sight of a field of sheep is one of my favourite things during my Sunday morning walks. To celebrate it I adapted the chicken design on pages 102–105 to make a sheep.

Materials

- 50 cm (19½ in) square of medium-weight natural calico
- A4 piece of cotton wadding
- Polyester fibre filling (can be left-over bits of wadding)
- Small plastic bag of grit, securely fastened.

Below:

The sheep we encounter on our Sunday morning walk always like to strike a pose when they have their photo taken.

Right:
This 'Shabby Sheep' was made
using a method similar to the
'Calico Chick' with an apron made
out of an old embroidered tray
cloth. See page 110 for details).

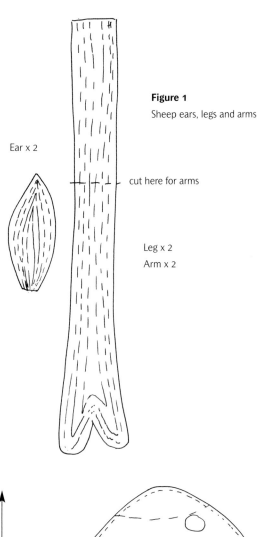

Figure 1

Sheep ears, legs and arms

Ear x 2

cut here for arms

Leg x 2
Arm x 2

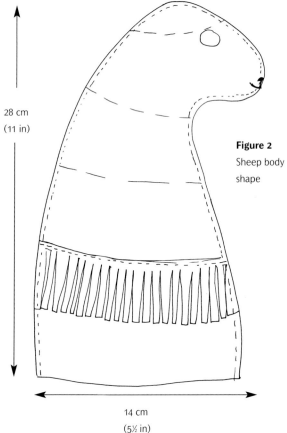

28 cm
(11 in)

Figure 2
Sheep body
shape

14 cm
(5½ in)

1. Cut an A3 piece of calico and draw two ears, two legs and two arms on one half (see figure 1).

2. Place the A4 piece of wadding on one side and fold the calico over the wadding to make it into a sandwich. Stitch up and down in lines as drawn on the pattern.

3. Cut all the shapes out within ½ cm (¼ in) of the stitch lines.

4. Dip the cut-out shapes into a mixture of a cup of strong black tea and a squirt of PVA. Squeeze the shapes and leave to dry.

5. Cut out two of the sheep body shapes in figure 2 (seam allowance are included)

6. Cut 2 calico strips of 12 cm (5 in) wide and 70 cm (28 in) long, fold in half lengthways and iron. Cut snips about 6mm (¼ in) apart, cutting to within 1.5 cm (¾ in) of the fold.

7. Stitch these lengths of 'fur' on the lines marked on the body pattern. Attach arms, ears and buttons (for the eyes) on each side of the body before stitching both body parts together, leaving a frayed edge. There is no need to turn it.

8. Stuff the body with the fibre filling but leave space at the bottom to insert the little bag of grit; this will help the sheep to sit up. Pin the base together with the seams meeting opposite together and with a leg inserted at each end. Machine stitch.

9. Make the apron as for the chicken design (see page 107) and embroider the mouth and nose by hand.

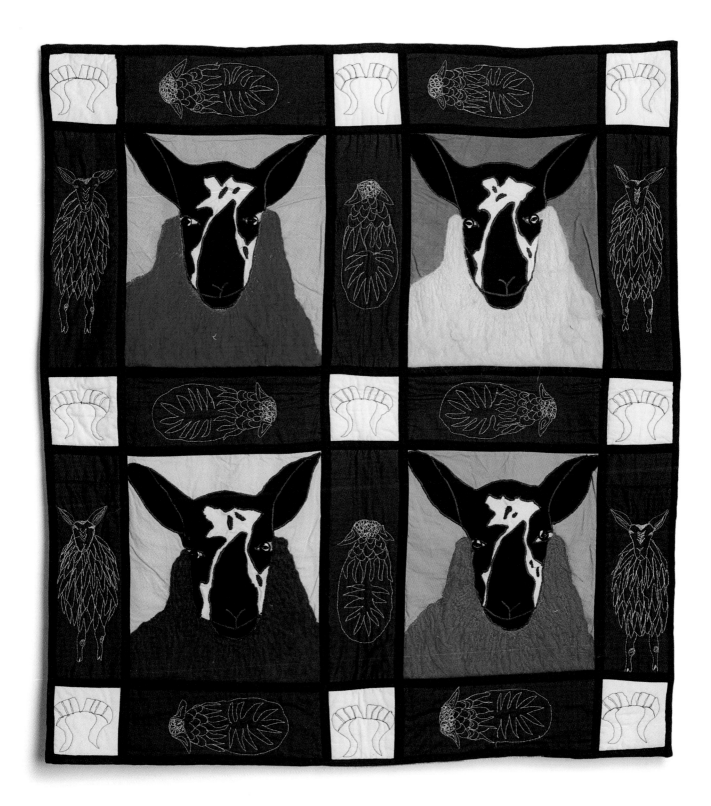

Above:
'Sheep the Warhol Way', a quilted
wallhanging by Liske Berlyn.

6 IDEAS FOR DIFFERENT MATERIALS

Most of the time we work with soft fabrics and textiles, either made from natural products, such as cotton, linen, hemp or wool, or the man-made fabrics, such as polyester, nylon and plastics. In addition, many of the items we make are displayed inside our houses or galleries. Nowadays, however, there is also a very strong emphasis on merging the boundaries between inside and the outside, giving us the need to create art with materials that are suitable for display inside or out. Every summer, there are more quilt exhibitions with work displayed outside, often in lovely gardens or parks.

Although these exhibitions are scheduled for summertime, this does not always mean that the weather conditions stick to their summer theme, so the displays have to withstand all kinds of weather, which in the United Kingdom can mean anything from severe hailstorms to days of glorious sunshine.

Each piece in a quilt display has to consist of at least two layers, but the type of material used for the layers can be anything, ranging from ordinary cotton to plastic, polyester or metals. Of course, work created for a summer outdoor display can be shown all through the year in your own garden, giving you a unique opportunity to brighten up an otherwise dull and boring winter garden.

Plastic

No doubt, the first thing you would think of using for outside work would be plastic and indeed this is a fantastic way to re-use all those plastic carrier bags that are so environmentally unfriendly. These are easy to cut and stitch. They come in a whole spectrum of colours and will withstand any weather conditions quite happily. I recently came across a lady who had used plastic carrier bags almost in the same way as she would have used cotton fabrics and made gorgeous squares, using the traditional folding method and stitching her lighter pieces onto a foundation of a stronger plastic. Using this method, you can create a very weather-resistant little hanging or tablecloth or recycle the plastic into another sturdy carrier bag.

Right:
Award-winning window-hanging 'Bluebells' made with transparent layers of polyester organza, appliquéd shapes of trees and leaves finished off with a layer of fine tulle. It was machine stitched and finally areas were burned away with a soldering iron.

Left:
Patchwork block made by folding squares cut out of plastic carrier bags and cat food packaging.

Right:
Detail of 'Bluebells' (see
previous page).

Polyester Sheer

The next material on my list is polyester sheer organza. These fabrics also come in all colours and can be layered, burned and stitched with the greatest of ease (as shown in the 'Bluebells' on page 113 and the detail on the left). The rain won't have too much of an effect on them because they dry so quickly and, being sheer, they offer you the advantage of transparency!

Lutradur

Another favourite of mine is Lutradur. The first piece I produced for an outdoor display was made of Lutradur, painted with acrylic paint. This is really PVA glue with colour pigment added to it, which is like adding another plastic coating. Lutradur stitches easily and with no fraying edgings, making it a real contender for a hard-wearing outdoor display. Lutradur can also be used to make larger versions of dragonflies, butterflies or even flying seagulls!

Cotton

Coloured cotton fabrics will withstand a fair amount of weather, but in time the colours will run and bleach in the sunshine, rips will fray and so on. A cotton piece may demonstrate the ravages of time and climate, but perhaps the result is not always pretty.

Left:
'Dutch Landscape' wallhanging
with appliqué on painted
Lutradur.

Wood

This is probably not the first thing that would spring to mind as a material that you can stitch, but walking along a beach in France I started to collect bits of driftwood, especially the pieces that had that salty, aged look. Collecting driftwood became quite contagious and soon visiting friends were bringing all kinds of oddly-shaped treasures back to me from their seaside trips. I played around with these for a bit and discovered I could use a drill as my sewing needle, drilling holes into each piece of wood. My husband found a solid chunk of tree trunk to use as a base for a piece of work and I bought a thin metal rod for my thread from the local DIY store.

Using a drill bit slightly larger than my metal rod, I drilled a hole about 10 cm (4 in) deep in the centre of the base, into which I placed the rod. I used the bigger pieces of wood to give the piece a solid base and then arranged the smaller pieces, interspersing them with some small pebbles also found on the beach. These were quite soft, so it was easy to drill holes in them with a concrete drill bit. The stones add a bit of contrast, not only in texture but in shape as well.

The top piece of wood reminded us of the head of an ostrich, so the whole shape was more-or-less based on creating a bird-like animal. I placed him in the shrubs, where the setting evening sun catches him as he gently sways in the winds.

He is a sculpture, but in my mind he's also a quilt: the pieces of wood with the pebbles are my layers of fabric; the drill is my needle, and the rod is the thread that holds it all together.

A hanging version of this shape can easily be made, using metal wire to thread the pieces of wood together.

A stone interpretation stands outside my studio. Drilling through the stone with a masonry drill bit was harder, but well worth the effort.

Metals

Metals are another material often used for sculpture, but not very often for quilts. Recycling drink cans is a brilliant way to use a material that is already coloured commercially. The cans can be layered with plastic to achieve the required two layers and of course there is no problem with fraying here either.

Right:
'Big Bird' was made by 'stitching' together pieces of driftwood and rocks using an electric drill as a needle and and a metal spike as a thread.

Project: Leaves and Grasses

In the autumn, you can use the leaves to print and bleach with: they are all there, just waiting to be picked up so you can 'do something with them'. During a walk in the woods last autumn, I took a carrier bag and picked up leaves in as many colours as I could find, taking them all from one particular sycamore tree. With them, I made this wreath to hang on my new front door.

I did not dry the leaves first, as they would have become too brittle to stitch. Instead, I waited until I had finished the wreath before pressing it to dry the leaves.

Right:
A collection of fresh autumn leaves are stitched together with a big needle and strong thread, overlapping them to form a circle.

Right:
The circle of leaves is then glued – using a glue gun – onto a ring cut out of cardboard.

1. Out of cardboard, I cut a circle with a diameter of about 37.5 cm (15 in) and cut another circle, about 7.5 cm (3 in) in diameter, from the centre. I used a large and a smaller dinner plate to draw the circles. Alternatively, use one of the wire wreaths that are available from garden centres, winding strips of fabric or wadding around it, to stitch into.

2. I sorted and placed the leaves so they overlapped each other, filling the cardboard circle. I then stitched them to each other by hand with a simple large running stitch, using a biggish needle and some strong cotton thread. It's easier to sew them in a long line, but while stitching you need to keep placing the string of leaves onto the cardboard template to check that they fit onto the round shape. When the circle is complete, join the two ends and finish the thread off at the back.

3. Using a glue gun, attach a ribbon at the top of the cardboard circle and then glue the circle of leaves onto the cardboard!

4. Next, dry the wreath between some sheets of newspaper with something heavy on top for a couple of days and then spray it with hair lacquer to preserve it against the wet. My wreath lasted quite well, although I had to press it every so often to flatten it again.

5. To make a more permanent wreath, the leaves can be cut from Lutradur with a soldering iron and then painted in a range of autumn colours. Alternatively, you could bond some autumn fabrics together with Bondaweb, and then cut and stitch the leaves before making them into a wreath.

Left:
The wreath is ready to hang
on the door.

7 FINISHING TOUCHES

When the main part of your work is complete, it is very important to give some careful consideration as to how to finish the edges. This is especially important if you are entering your work in a competition, but it is also essential for your own satisfaction that the quilt is finished with the same care and attention with which you made it.

These days there are no hard and fast rules, especially with art quilts, but the finish should really be in harmony with the quilt itself. If you visit a quilt show, you could concentrate on this particular aspect of the quilts and take some close-up pictures (if allowed), accompanied by short written notes on different finishing techniques that might be of interest to you. I have included some of the most obvious and interesting ones that I have come across.

A Traditional Finish

The traditional way of finishing your quilt, especially if it is one that will get a lot of use, is to bind it with a double binding that has been cut on the bias of the fabric. For those pieces that are hung on the wall, a single binding is often used. The binding can be in a contrasting fabric or one that blends in.

First measure your quilt widthways, taking measurements across the top, middle and bottom and then calculating the average width. Do the same for the length. Cut your binding – 3 cm (1¼ in) wide for a single or 5 cm (2 in) wide for a double binding. Cut and join sufficient strips to make a length twice the average width and twice the average length, plus some extra for the corners.

Left:
Single binding using different coloured fabrics.

Right:
Invisible binding with inserted folded triangles.

Fold the binding in half lengthways and mark the centre point with a pin, then match this with the halfway mark on your quilt. Add 1 cm (½ in)at each end for the corners, then attach the binding at each end, leaving 1 cm (½ in) to fold in at the corners and pin in between, stretching the binding slightly if needed.

Stitch to the right side of your quilt with the machine. The first corner does not need folding over and the 1 cm (½ in) seam allowance can be snipped off, but for the next three corners you will need to fold over the 1 cm (½ in) seam allowance and then fold the binding over to the back of the quilt. Pin and stitch by hand.

Don't forget to sign and date your quilt! To give your binding a more contemporary feel, why not add a few inches of coloured fabric that you have used in the quilt itself and insert these randomly in your binding before cutting it to the required lengths. This brings the binding and the quilt nicely together. To add further interest, you might incorporate a few beads in some blanket stitches here and there or make some long stitches, overlapping the binding and the quilt.

Invisible Binding

This is very similar to the traditional binding and is best done with a single thickness. Cut your binding about 3 cm (1¼ in) deep. Calculate and cut the correct length as before. Pin and stitch the binding to the right side of the quilt. You could insert small folded triangles or other shapes in-between the edges of the quilt (as shown below) and the binding before stitching the binding to the quilt. When you fold the binding towards the back, these additions will form an interesting sculpted edge. Fold all of the binding to the back. Pin and stitch by hand.

Top:
Quick-machined binding.

Right:
Sides are straight stitched close to
the edge and left to fray.

Left:
The white binding has been folded
over to the back, then machine
quilted, whilst the pink edge is a
traditional binding, hand stitched
on the back and with a few beads
added within a blanket stitch.

Quick-machined Binding

This binding is suitable for sample pieces or finishing off bags. Cut strips of 3 cm (1¼ in). Fold and iron 0.5 cm (¼ in) on one side. Stitch the other side onto the back of your work with a 0.5 cm (¼ in) seam allowance, then fold the ironed-under edge to the front, pin and stitch.

Fold-over Binding

If you have a generous helping of your top layer left, you can straighten this with a rotary cutter, then cut back your wadding and lining fabric, iron over a 6 mm (¼ in) seam and fold this towards the back. Pin and stitch.

'Bagging it'

If you have made a real mess of your back and do not want this to show – the only solution is back it. Cut a piece of fabric the same size as the quilt. With right sides together, pin it to the quilt and then machine stitch with a 0.5 cm (¼ in) seam allowance all around the edges, leaving a gap big enough to turn the whole thing through. Turn the quilt and backing right side out; close the gap by hand stitching, and add some hand or machine topstitching to keep edges in place. I used this method for the dress quilt on page 45, as a bra filled with some wadding had to be inserted after the quilting was done.

Raw Edges

You may choose to have raw edges around small items, such as postcards. If you have used a few raw edges in your quilt top, it might be appropriate to leave the outer sides gently frayed as well.

You can stay-stitch around the edge a couple of times with a thread that either contrasts or blends in. I would advise using a walking foot! To finish, cut off the excess fabric to within 6 mm (¼ in) of your stitching.

Again, a few blanket stitches might add a colourful finishing touch.

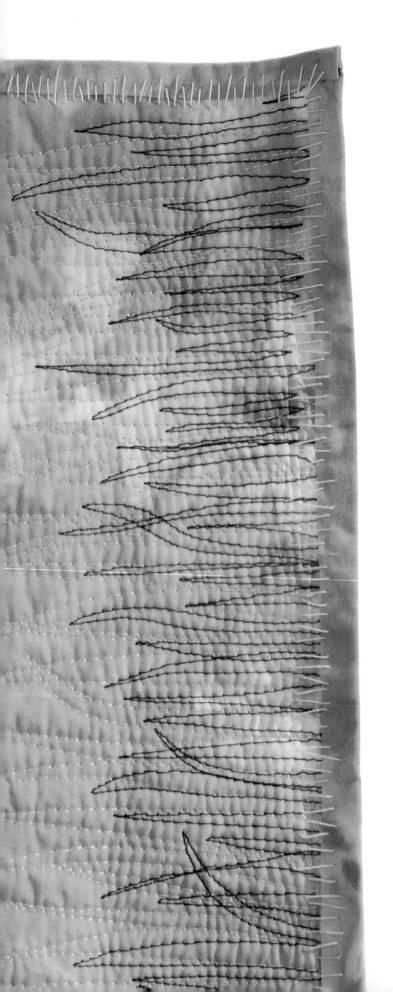

Dyed Wadding

You have to plan well in advance for this one. *Before you start your quilt*, dye a cotton or 80/20 wadding in a colour that co-ordinates with your quilt design and, when constructing your quilt, rip your side edges to fray neatly in a straight line. When all is quilted, you only have to straighten out the wadding (which looks very much like felt when dyed) with a rotary cutter and long ruler.

Fold-over and Fuse with Bondaweb

This is a novel way of finishing an edge and I saw this on one of the journal quilt displays. Cut a 2 cm (¾ in) strip of binding and iron a 1.5 cm (½ in) strip of Bondaweb onto the back of this, leaving a narrow edge clear of Bondaweb. Leave the paper on and stitch to the back of the quilt, following the paper edge. Then take off the paper, fold the binding towards the front of the quilt and iron into place. A simple decorative straight stitch can be added by hand. Because the edges are backed with Bondaweb they should not fray.

Satin Stitch

Satin stitch is an ideal and quick way to finish small projects like the postcards. Choose a thread in a colour that suits the design, use the same thread in the bobbin and set your machine to zigzag and the stitch length to ½ or less. Sample the stitching first before sewing onto your quilt. Start about 3 cm (1¼ in) from a corner and stop just short of the corner with the needle down right into the corner of the quilt, turn your work 45 degrees, sew two or three stitches, turn again, sew two or three stitches, turn again and continue down the next side and stop short of the corner again.

Left:
Sample showing folded edges that have been fused with Bondaweb.

Right:

This postcard has been cut neatly and finished off with tight satin stitch.

Right:

Here dyed wadding is showing underneath the quilt top.

FURTHER INFORMATION

SUPPLIERS

Art Van Go
The Studios
1 Stevenage Road
Knebworth
Hertfordshire SG3 6RE
Tel: 01438 814946
www.artvango.co.uk

Quilt und Textilkunst
Sebastianplatz 4
Munich
0049 (0) 89 230 77401
www.quiltundtextilkunst.de

Dye suppliers:
Kemtex Colours
Chorley Business and Technology Park
Euxton Lane
Chorley
Lancashire PR7 6TE
Tel.: 01257 230 220
www.kemtex.co.uk
or www.omegadyes.co.uk

Fabric supplier:
Whaleys (Bradford) Ltd.
Harris Court
Great Horton
Bradford BD7 4EQ
Tel.: 01274 521 309

Thermofax screen supplier:
www.thermofaxscreens.co.uk
www.angiehughes.com

Fine-tipped soldering irons supplier:
Margaret Beal Embroidery
01264 365102
burning.issues@margaretbeal.co.uk

Rulers, threads and other quilt supplies in the UK:
www.equilter.com
(Quilting threads, tulle and other quilt supplies)

Ineke Berlyn
www.inekeberlyn.com
ine@inekeberlyn.com

www.creativegrids.com

For courses and workshops on fabric dyeing and decoration techniques in UK:
Committed to Cloth
Leslie Morgan and Claire Benn
www.committedtocloth.com

SOCIETIES AND GROUPS

The Quilters Guild
www.quiltersguild.org.uk

The Embroiderers Guild
www.embroiderersguild.com

The Textile Society
www.textilesociety.org.uk

MAGAZINES AND JOURNALS

Selvedge
PO Box 40038
London N6 5UW
www.selvedge.org

Quilting Arts Magazine & *Cloth Paper Scissors* Magazine
PO Box 685
Stow.
MA
USA
www.quiltingartsllc.com

The Textile Directory
Word4Word Publishers
Tel.: 0870 220 2423
www.thetextiledirectory.com

INDEX